SUPERFLEX

Ms. Olympia's Guide to Building a Strong & Sexy Body

SUPERFLEX

Ms. Olympia's Guide to Building a Strong & Sexy Body

By **CORINNA EVERSON**
with **Jeff Everson**

CONTEMPORARY
BOOKS, INC.
CHICAGO ■ NEW YORK

Library of Congress Cataloging-in-Publication Data

Everson, Corinna.
  Superflex: Ms. Olympia's guide to building a
strong & sexy body.

   1. Bodybuilding for women.   I. Everson, Jeff.
II. Title.
GV546.6.W64E9   1987   646.7'5   86-32997
ISBN 0-8092-4865-4 (pbk.)

Published by Contemporary Books, Inc.
180 North Michigan Avenue, Chicago, Illinois 60601
Manufactured in the United States of America
Library of Congress Catalog Card Number: 8-32997
International Standard Book Number: 0-8092-4865-4

Published simultaneously in Canada by Beaverbooks, Ltd.
195 Allstate Parkway, Valleywood Business Park
Markham, Ontario L3R 4T8 Canada

To our mothers.
Thank you for the courage and foresight to be individuals.

CONTENTS

Author's Note   vi
Acknowledgments   vii
1   Bodybuilding and the New Sensuality   1
2   Bionic Blood   11
3   Bodybuilding Basics   23
4   Why Diet is a Dirty Word   41
5   Slim Thighs and Buttocks   53
6   Tight Tummies   63
7   Shapely Breasts   73
8   Powerful Arms   89
9   Sexy Shoulders   105
10   Beautiful Back   117
11   Enviable Legs   131
12   Heart and Soul   147
13   Questions and Answers   165
14   The Complete Ms. Olympia Workout Program   179
     Parting Thoughts   195
     The Superflex Glossary   197
     Appendices   203
     Index   207

AUTHOR'S NOTE

I advise any person who wants to undertake a program of exercise to undergo a thorough exercise stress test and physical evaluation with a physician. Not only is this a good indicator of your overall level of fitness and a measure of your need for exercise, it also is beneficial to have a complete physical checkup once a year, no matter what shape you *think* you are in! People with known health problems should consult with their doctors before undertaking any physical program outlined in this book.

ACKNOWLEDGMENTS

To women with enough individuality to fulfill their dreams and desires.

To Jeff, for your constant guidance, but most of all, for instilling within me the confidence enabling me to realize my potential.

To our wonderful parents and families.

To Joe Weider, Trainer of Champions. Thank you for ignoring the "so-called" experts and promoting bodybuilding anyway. Also, for your generous contribution of photographs.

To Harry Langdon, Mike Neveux, Paul Goode, Darrell Peterson, Dick Zimmerman, and Ken Merfeld, great photographers, but more importantly, great friends.

To Jo Ellen Krumm, copy-editing wizard.

To John Traetta and Contemporary Books, who actualized the *Superflex* concept.

SUPERFLEX

Ms. Olympia's Guide to Building a Strong & Sexy Body

1
BODYBUILDING AND THE NEW SENSUALITY

It is a safe bet that the majority of women in our society would like to be more fit, sexier, and more beautiful. Beauty, though, is a commodity difficult to define. Beauty is greatly ascribed to and admired, but no one has ever satisfactorily described it.

Is beauty simply a pretty face, an endearing smile, or enchanting, mysterious eyes? Is it an elusive Raquel Welch full-bodied figure or the slimmer Cher look so popular in the ritzy world of haute couture? Might beauty be represented by Cybill Shepherd's golden hair glimmering in the moonlight?

Undeniably, the cliche that beauty is in the eye of the beholder is true, but that doesn't prevent thousands of women from wanting to become sexier or, as they perceive themselves, more beautiful than they are. With all the perceptions of beauty and sexiness, what's a woman to do?

BODYBUILDING FITNESS: MY STANDARD OF SENSUALITY

A sexy woman is someone who has a figure that catches your eye in a positive way. Usually, the so-called sexy woman is sleek, curvacious, and physically charismatic. She has a certain look. Most models, who make a living off their sex appeal, spend hours and hours practicing their sexy looks. Almost everyone agrees, in our culture, neither an overweight nor an underweight woman has much sex appeal.

Sex appeal and beauty require body curves in the right places. They require a certain attitude as well. Bodybuilding, because it pares away fat and increases muscle tone (putting life and shape into your natural curves), is capable of enhancing every woman's sensuality. You don't have to be a competitive bodybuilder, just train with some form of progressive resistance to enhance your muscle tone and add shapely curves and new energy to your life.

With your newfound form comes greater self-confidence. As you begin to shape up—losing inches here and gaining inches there—others will soon begin to notice. You'll bask in a ray of compliments, heads will turn, and your hard work will seem more than worthwhile. I certainly wasn't the first to reshape my body through bodybuilding and I won't be the last. Women everywhere are redesigning their bodies and are reaping the benefits and becoming healthier, sexier, happier with their lives.

In many of the hot fashion boutiques, the words *shape*, *firmness*, *physical beauty*, *strength*, and *sexy athleticism* are the new slogans. These words describe the new models, the real images behind the lenses of the fashion photographers. Look at our current female sexual ideals: Linda Evans, Raquel Welch, Mariel Hemingway, Heather Thomas, Cybill Shepherd, Victoria Principal, Jane Fonda, and Farrah Fawcett. These women are all athletic. No longer does sexy mean thin. Sexy means healthy and fit, the new beauty!

Total beauty and healthy, fit sensuality can be attained through bodybuilding. So can strength and advanced muscle tone. Bodybuilding is the only exercise that really changes your shape. When you improve your shape, you improve your sexual attractiveness. You become happier and more confident with yourself, and more successful in all facets of life.

Why is bodybuilding so unique? Well, with almost every other exercise form, you don't get a complete makeover. I used to jog up to 10 miles a day. My lungs became more efficient and I suppose my heart was stronger, but I also got my share of injuries, muscle pulls, sore shins and feet, and a dog bite or two! Running didn't do anything for my muscle shape, except for my calf muscles. Bodybuilding, though, can change you from top to bottom.

Bodybuilding has produced more cases of metamorphosis than any surgical or dietary technique. I feel beautifully fit, which is why I continue to work out so hard. Muscle tone gives more zest to my step and more life to my feminine curves. And, when I'm in my competitive stage for bodybuilding, it gives me the muscle and definition I need to win in competition. Bodybuilding has given me three Ms. Olympia victories.

FEMININITY AND SENSUALITY

Bodybuilding enhances strength, increases your muscle tone, and pares away fat. It's virtually impossible for the average woman to build really large muscles. My muscles are larger than average, but I've been a competitive athlete for 16 years and I have been bodybuilding twice a day for seven years! The average woman who bodybuilds improves her muscle tone and loses fat. She does not grow a moustache or bulge out like Hercules. Bodybuilding does improve your shape and muscle tone, and elevates femininity rather than diminishes it.

It seems that every time I go to an exhibition somewhere around the country, a woman wanting to start bodybuilding ap-

proaches me after my appearance and exclaims joyfully that I have totally shattered the image she held that I was going to be muscle-bound and very unfeminine looking. They go on to say they are convinced and will immediately take up bodybuilding!

Naturally, this makes me feel pretty darn good, but her concern is that of many women interested in starting a bodybuilding program. Muscle cells are like brain cells. They're *meant* to be used. It's common to find men ogling over women track and field athletes and gymnasts. Why? Because their bodies are sleek and tight. They possess an athletic sexiness. Bodybuilding can make any woman look like a well-conditioned athlete.

My Theory of Relativity

Everything is relative. Once you understand that you will never develop muscles as large as the average man your fears will be eliminated and you'll be on your way to becoming the woman you have always wanted to be.

Think about it. In my case, after years of grueling workouts, twice a day, my biceps are still smaller than those of an *untrained* man! I'm pretty strong, too. I can bench press my weight easily, all 148 pounds, but my husband Jeff bench presses close to 600 pounds! So much for relativity!

We all need to free ourselves of these silly notions. You won't become masculine from bodybuilding, but you will become more shapely, sexy, and fit. And it doesn't matter what your genetic makeup is, either, because bodybuilding will redesign your body from head to toe, as I'm about to show you.

MUSCLE MYTHS

Bodybuilding continues to be full of tall tales. Of course, the tallest of all is that you lose your femininity when you work with weights. Nonsense. You can still be sensitive, emotional, loving, caring, and intuitive, and keep all the sexual characteristics that define femininity.

Big muscles are a masculine trait. Males have much more testosterone than women. This is a hormone that allows a trained man to develop big muscles. Since women do not have much testosterone, it's very hard for us

to build large muscles. The physiological makeup of a woman won't allow it. When you work out, the typical response will be to lose fat and gain muscle tone. And, just because you bodybuild, this does *not* imply that you are, or have to be, a competitive bodybuilder.

I can point to myself as an example. It's a misconception that you will "bulk up" the moment you pick up a dumbbell.

When I graduated from high school I weighed 143 pounds. Today, some 10 years later, I usually weigh 148 pounds. I think most women would settle for a 5-pound weight gain their first 10 years out of high school! In 1986, the night of my third Ms. Olympia victory, I weighed 146 pounds. Over those 10 years of hard training, I redesigned my body. I haven't added an ounce of fat since high school. I still wear my high school jeans. I've shaped up, lost fat, and improved my muscle tone. I feel much better, too. Bodybuilding can do the same for you!

MUSCLE INTO FAT? FAT INTO MUSCLE?

Like the alchemists of long ago who could not turn base metal into gold, neither can you turn muscle into fat or fat into muscle. Having good muscle tone implies that you train. No one has it *unless* they train.

When a long-distance jogger stops running, her heart rate creeps back up, her blood cholesterol may jump a bit, and her blood pressure may go up a point or two. When anyone stops training, they lose a great portion of what they had gained in the first place. A muscular athlete who stops training loses muscle tone, but she does not automatically become fat unless she continues to eat as she did when she was in heavy training.

So why do people think muscle turns to fat when you quit? Like the question of femininity, they just don't know the facts. When muscle atrophies (gets smaller) without training stress, and you do not cut back your calories commensurately, fat can envelop the muscle. To prevent this, if you do stop training, simply cut back on the consumption of fat calories from your food. To keep from gaining body fat, eat less fat! Muscles never "turn" to fat, they just get smaller when you stop working them!

MENSTRUATION AND BODYBUILDING

Some people think that bodybuilding is not a good idea for women because they are afraid that women who exercise will end up with damaged sexual organs. This is not true. I recall a doctor who knew little about exercise told me that if I continued to jog I would progressively loosen up the ligaments supporting my uterus. I would in turn have difficulty with childbirth should I become pregnant. I have read nothing that supports this contention and I know many women

who have jogged regularly and given birth without any such difficulties.

In fact, the opposite appears to be true. A study of 700 mothers showed that those who exercised regularly before delivery had shorter labors and *easier* deliveries. Their need for cesarean delivery was far less than their nonexercising counterparts. The reason? Better muscle tone in their abdominal muscles.

I am frequently questioned by women who undertake a vigorous bodybuilding program and all of a sudden their periods stop. While some women actually enjoy it when their periods stop, others are quite concerned about this.

Evidently, vigorous exercise, whether it be bodybuilding, dancing, or running, disrupts the normal menstrual cycle.

Doctors say that low body fat levels, induced by exercise, trigger hormonal changes in our bodies that cause this disruption. I notice that when my own body fat dips to the 10% level, my periods can stop or become much lighter. When I stop training for a while on a layoff, my periods normalize.

Any change in your menstrual flow because of exercise is only temporary. The American College of Sports Medicine states, "Disruption of the menses exists with female athletes, but there's no evidence indicating that this is harmful to the female reproductive system."

BASIC NUTRITION AND SUPPLEMENTS

Contrary to popular belief, most bodybuilders do not gulp down hundreds of vitamin pills and foul-smelling protein concoctions all day long. Furthermore, smart bodybuilders don't starve themselves to gain muscle definition, either. Starving yourself won't help you achieve your goals, and certainly won't win you any physique contests.

I don't believe in the typical calorie-controlled diet. It's too rigid and limiting. Yet, good health, stunning sex appeal, and vibrant beauty are related to nutrition. To look good and to feel good, you must eat good. Billy Crystal's Fernando says, "It's better to look good than to feel good, darling." However, I'd say they're both important.

All people interested in fitness should eat wholesome (and quite low in calories) foods such as breads, pasta, fresh fruits, salads, lean meats (in small quantities), and all kinds of vegetables. I can eat as much of these foods as I want without worrying about putting on excess weight. These foods (essentially carbohydrates) give you a lot of energy without adding a lot of needless calories.

My diet is balanced, consisting of a mixture of these foods. It is high in natural carbohydrates, low in fat and salt, and moderate in protein. I really watch what I eat only the last few weeks before a physique contest and even then I'm not too concerned about it. That is because I eat the right foods year-round.

Personally, I'm not fond of taking a lot of vitamins and minerals or extra protein powder. I will do this before a contest where the stress on my body is very high or when I'm selectively cutting back on certain foodstuffs. (In my chapter on nutrition, "Diet Is a Dirty Word," I give a delicious and detailed program that will satisfy your tummy and complement your bodybuilding training.)

Ergogenic Aids

Ergogenic means work-enhancing. Many food supplements (vitamins and minerals, etc.) are advertised to be work-enhancing. Some might be, especially if you are deficient in some essential nutrients to begin with. Extra work and stress require that you counterbalance their effects through good nutrition, especially by consuming more carbohydrates.

Anabolic steroids (a chemical drug with properties similar to the major male hormone, testosterone) are work-enhancing aids. They are only available with a medical prescription and are dangerous. Besides being potentially harmful to your liver, heart, and kidneys, they have potential virilizing (making you more male-like) effects.

While it's true that some bodybuilders probably have experimented with anabolic steroids, far more have achieved success without them. Steroids are used primarily to build mass, but pure muscle size is *not* the main criteria for success in women's bodybuilding. Symmetry, shape, and proportion are more important, and are not enhanced through steroid use.

Just because an athlete is able to develop larger and more defined musculature does not indict him or her as a user of steroids, nor does it imply, if they have, that steroids are the *major* reason for their development. Hard work and correct nutrition make champions, not anabolic steroids! Today, in most of the major women's competitions, tests are given to make sure that any of the competitors who are using or have recently used steroids are forced to sit out that competition. This is in the interest of making the sport safe.

ANATOMY IS NOT DESTINY

It's no secret that there are physical differences between men and women. Vive la difference! The physiological differences between the sexes hold both advantages and disadvantages when bodybuilding.

Women have wider and heavier pelvic bones and thus a lower center of gravity. Women tend to store more body fat in their lower extremities as well. Many, many women come to me hoping for some help in shedding excess weight from their thighs and hips. Being slim and trim in these areas means sex appeal to most women. Since it's so important, I devote a separate chapter to it ("Slim Thighs and Buttocks").

Just because you currently have heavy hips doesn't mean you can't slim them, firm them, and develop far greater sex appeal and muscle tone. Granted, it's harder, but it can be done! On the other side of the coin, there's an advantage. Because women have larger leg bones, they can develop great leg strength. Proportionately, when you correct for men's heavier body weights, women are as strong as men in their legs. This is why, in the lighter weight classes, some women can lift as much as men in the squat lift. Women with larger hip bones can still become outstanding bodybuilders.

LOSING FAT: GETTING SEXIER!

If you asked the average woman what would make them sexier, nine out of ten would probably say, "Losing fat." Being overweight conjures up images of neither beauty nor sexiness. In fact, just hearing the word fat makes most women shudder. It's funny, even though we spend half our lives trying to get rid of fat, not all of it is so bad. On the average, most unathletic women range from 18% to 35% body fat. Of course, female bodybuilders and other athletes have much less body fat.

My body fat is about 12%. Some other high-level female bodybuilders have gone as low as 5% to 8%, but I don't think this is healthy. At this level of body fat, you do not have enough fullness to look healthy and curvaceous. Women interested in recreational fitness should keep their body fat between 15% and 20%, while competitive bodybuilders should stay between 10% and 15%.

We do carry more fat naturally. We have more essential fat in our internal organs. Essential fat cannot be dieted or trained away, nor should it be! Experts say that up to 10% of the fat differences between the sexes is due to our higher essential fat.

Another kind of fat is known as storage fat. Storage fat lies underneath our skin, between our cells, and surrounds all our organs (liver, uterus, kidneys, heart, etc.). Storage fat protects and insulates. It warms us in winter, gives us year-round energy, and, together with muscle tone, provides us

with our feminine curves. Suffice it to say that our higher fat level makes it difficult to gain definition for competition. But if it's not in excess, fat adds to a woman's sensuality and beauty.

How Do We Respond to Exercise?

Exercise, particularly bodybuilding, can do anything you want it to. You can shape up, improve your tone and curves, lose fat or add muscle, and become stronger and more fit. I respond to bodybuilding just like my husband does, only I can't get as big or strong. I don't have the hormones for huge muscles and my skeletal size and leverage dictates that my strength and power is less.

Don't be surprised when you start bodybuilding if you actually gain a pound or two. Remember, the mirror is far more valuable than the scale in measuring your progress. Muscle is heavier than fat. Even though you lose some fat, you may tip the scales the other way! Women *always* guess my weight at 130 pounds. Most are flabbergasted when I tell them I'm 150 pounds. If you are in good shape, you don't carry your weight, it carries you!

After a year or so of training, you'll find many people asking you how much weight you've lost even if you've stayed exactly the same! You'll also find that you do not continue gaining weight. It's much easier to lose fat than it is to gain muscle. Unless you are underweight, most women bodybuilders *never* gain more than 10 pounds of *solid* muscle no matter how many years they work out! It's not so easy.

PUT SOME HEART INTO IT!

I'm sure some of you reading this have heard that weightlifting is bad for your heart. This is simply ridiculous. Provided your heart is healthy, any exercise, even static isometrics, is better than no exercise.

Your heart is a muscle, too, and favorably responds to exercise. With bodybuilding, you lift a submaximal weight a number of times. Then you rest and repeat this procedure. Your heart rate goes up, you perspire, and your breathing rate increases. All of which means that your heart is working to pump blood throughout your body. Thus, it's getting exercised.

Bodybuilders not only want to improve their appearance through better muscle tone, they want to improve their heart efficiency as well, and they can do so through circuit training. With a circuit system you do a number of exercises, all for different parts of your body, one right after another, without any rest in between exercises. Your whole program should last about an hour.

This type of bodybuilding training will give your heart and lungs a very good workout.

The Wizard of Oz said, "Hearts won't be perfect until they can't be broken." They also won't be perfect unless they keep ticking for a long time without stopping prematurely, causing untimely deaths! Heart disease is still the major cause of death in adults in America today. A bodybuilding lifestyle coupled with a good nutrition program help prevent heart disease from attacking you.

The average woman has a resting heart rate of 82 beats per minute. A man's average is 72 beats per minute. Generally, the slower your heart rate and the quicker your heart rate returns to normal after exercise, the better shape you are in. My resting

heart rate is in the upper fifties so I feel pretty good about that. The slow heart rate means your heart works less to send blood around your body. Women have faster heart rates because we have less oxygen-carrying hemoglobin in our blood. Therefore, our hearts beat faster to make up for this. Remember, there are only two situations when your heart beats fast that are good for you: one, right after (and during) exercise; and two, when a handsome guy walks by and winks at you!

METABOLISM

Society constantly reinforces thinness, which is unfortunate. Many women have naturally slower metabolic rates and heavier bones, which makes it harder for them to keep trim. Generally, as smaller individuals, women do have slower metabolisms. Because women have less muscle, pound for pound, when compared to a man, women have slower metabolisms. This means that the fat we eat is more readily stored than burned as energy.

Enhanced muscle tone requires more calories. Bodybuilding adds muscle. Muscle burns calories, fat does not. This is why bodybuilding controls your weight so well, making you more fit, stronger, and sexier!

THE SUPERIOR SEX

Statistically, women outlive men. We live on the average 79 years, while men live only 70. Our higher estrogen levels protect us from heart disease, at least until menopause. Men's higher testosterone levels seem to work in the reverse. Studies show that when animals are given testosterone a high percentage develop heart disease and strokes compared to those that were not given testosterone. When the same animals are withdrawn from testosterone, their heart vessels return toward a healthy state, free of disease. Thus, the same testosterone that enables men to develop big muscles from bodybuilding can predispose them to a greater probability of heart disease. That's one of the reasons for a woman's longer lifespan. A noted anthropologist once wrote that women were really the stronger sex. Now that was a wise person!

Okay, ladies, it's now going to be up to you. I'm going to show you how to lose weight and improve your muscle tone, strength, and flexibility. Adhering to my program will allow you to redesign and create the figure that you've always wanted. You can even go into competitive bodybuilding training. It's all up to you. It's time for SUPERFLEX!

2
BIONIC BLOOD

On a chilly Midwestern spring night in April 1981, I had the most terrifying experience of my life. I was awakened by stabbing pains in my left leg. Even though my room was cool, I was soaked with clammy sweat. The pain was excruciating. I fumbled in the dark, finally finding the switch on my bedside lamp. I sat up and tossed back the covers. I couldn't believe my eyes. My left leg was completely swollen. It was twice the size of my right one.

I remember screaming. I must have hyperventilated because I passed out. When I came to, I was in my mother's car on the way to the Highland Park Hospital emergency room. My mother and stepfather had carried me from my bed downstairs to the car!

When I got to the hospital, doctors swarmed over me. They stuck needles and tubes in both arms and my left leg. I had no idea what was going on, only that I was scared to death. In hindsight, I was lucky I *didn't* know what was going on. I later learned I could've died right then and there. I had solid clots through three major veins

in my left leg. If any part of those clots had dislodged, it could have caused a heart attack or a stroke.

Three weeks before my trip to the hospital, I developed a dull ache in my groin. I was dieting and training for the 1981 Midwest Couples Bodybuilding Championships. I was running up to eight miles a day. Back then, the muscular but ultralean ripped-to-shreds look was in. I was under tremendous physical, mental, and emotional stress. I was working in downtown Chicago and was separated by 150 miles from my fiance, Jeff. I didn't like my job.

I don't know exactly why or how I developed the pain. I didn't pay much attention to it. Athletes learn to live with pain. I kept pushing. That was a big mistake.

The pain persisted. I finally went to my doctor, who told me I had a muscle pull. Neither Jeff nor I was satisfied with that so I visited a gynecologist. She also told me I had pulled a muscle deep in my abdominal area. That very night my leg clotted up.

At the hospital, the doctors told me I had bionic blood. For some reason they couldn't

11

regulate my blood-clotting time. The clots refused to dissipate. Finally, because I revealed my intentions to continue bodybuilding, the doctors tried a new drug, a powerful enzyme called Streptokinase. Today this is used to treat people who develop clots after heart attacks. The doctors call it medical Drano.

Whether it was time or the drug I don't know, but gradually the swelling receded. Jeff had left Madison, Wisconsin, and sat by my bed for 10 hours a day. He constantly encouraged me to believe in myself and to think positively. He told me that I could heal myself with the power of my mind if I could channel all my energy into positive thought. We both prayed a lot.

While I appeared cheerful on the outside, on the inside I was frightened. I had never been sick or hospitalized. Jeff knew I was depressed. He asked one of his wacky college friends to rent a Superman suit and visit me in the hospital. You should have heard the head nurse when she received a phone call from the downstairs security guard that the Man of Steel was there waiting to visit Corinna Kneuer. As a matter of fact, you should have seen their faces when he came upstairs to my room. I loved it.

Everyone treated me great. You know how everyone complains about hospital food. Well, I'm a big eater and I couldn't get enough. The cooks downstairs took a fancy to me because I kept complimenting them on their cuisine. They sent me extra portions all the time. Still, it wasn't enough and Jeff and my wonderful mother smuggled in ice cream and popcorn every night. Maybe all that food broke up the clots.

All this time (I was in intensive care for four weeks), the doctors warned that my bodybuilding career was probably over. They told me that I would develop varicose veins in my leg and bodybuilding might make them worse. They also told me they didn't know what had caused the clots.

Oh, there were a lot of theories about the cause, but no one could actually pin it down. I went to special hospitals for detailed blood molecule tests. One hospital found

I'm fading fast during the running leg of the Pentathlon Championships.

that there was a genetic problem in one of my clotting factors. I produced too much. They said my parents and sisters were also prone to fast blood clotting. Another hospital disagreed and failed to confirm their findings.

Since I wasn't using birth control pills and had no measurable family history of such clotting problems, one group of doctors said that an old muscle and connective tissue tear that I suffered years ago in track might have been the culprit. The leg injury had bothered me periodically. The doctors figured that the old scar tissue became inflamed when I started running again, training so hard and dieting. Together with the high level of personal stress I was under, it might have been responsible.

The scar tissue was aggravated and possibly enveloped small veins. I first developed phlebitis (inflammation of the veins—you remember phlebitis, Richard Nixon had it), then, when I kept going on it, clots set in.

Had I known that and rested with my leg elevated, I would never have developed clots.

When I got out of the hospital, I had one goal, to learn to walk again! The veins in my leg were badly scarred and it hurt to stand and walk. I lost 15 pounds in the hospital despite the voraciousness of my appetite. I lost muscle, almost all of it from my legs. I weighed a birdlike 128 pounds.

I started swimming because it didn't bother my leg and I knew it would help build my upper body back up. I made one lap the first day, but before I knew it, I was doing 100 laps nonstop. I began riding my bike and taking long leisurely walks. By the end of July, the doctors were amazed at my progress and gave me the go-ahead to bodybuild—but upper body only.

Jeff and I decided we'd enter the 1981 American Couples Championships in September in Las Vegas. We had placed third the year before and even though there were only two months until the show, it would give me a goal to work for.

HOW SWEET IT IS

Although I was dreadfully out of shape and light at 130 pounds, we won the contest! Just four months after getting out of intensive care, I was American champion with Jeff. I had made it back! To this day the victory in the 1981 Couples remains the sweetest and most rewarding.

I guess people don't realize all that we went through in winning this show. In addition to my blood clot and difficult rehabilitation, Jeff and I actually put our couples routine together through the mail! That's right, we made the poses up and wrote down all the little details of each pose and then memorized them. Remember, Jeff and I were 150 miles apart.

© Trix Rosen

What a feeling! Winning a national couples competition with my husband Jeff.

Only the actual two nights before the competition did we practice the lifts in our routine. Of course, I knew how to do them from my cheerleading background, but it still is a highly unusual way to learn a couples routine!

So, what happened when we actually competed? For some reason, the guy running the music tapes put on the wrong music when we were on stage! I mean this was a musical selection we had never heard before. I remember having this phony smile on my face and whispering to Jeff, "Jeff, that's not our music, whadda we do now?" Jeff looked at me and said, "Pose." It was one of those split-second decisions that you don't have time to think about. Anyway, we posed and pulled it off somehow. To this day, not too many people realize we won the American Championships posing to music we'd never heard before!

A LONG DAY'S JOURNEY INTO MIGHT!

I never thought my childhood back in Deerfield, Illinois, was all that unusual. Then again, not too many little girls have a mom who hotrods a school bus, and once set off a German stick bomb in the school's ventilation system and drove a race car!

My hunt for these Easter eggs was much easier than for the Ms. Olympia title.

I suppose it was my blessing that I was raised atypically. My father, a World War II rescue pilot, was shot down and spent time in an enemy prison camp. While he was there he taught prisoners the rudiments of gymnastics. To this day, at 63, he's an outstanding athlete.

Until I was out of high school my mom could beat me in arm-wrestling and hold her own with me in road races. You might say I was raised in an athletic family. Together with my two sisters, Cameo and Charmaigne, and several friends, we formed the "anti-femme" society. The anti-femme society might have been one of the first female liberation groups. You couldn't join our club if you ever planned on getting married or if you couldn't do everything the boys did!

My childhood idols were heroes, not heroines. Bomba, the Jungle Boy, Mighty Mouse, and Tarzan got my attention. Naturally, I started swimming and gymnastics when I was very young. I swam so much with our local club it's a wonder I don't have gills and webbed feet.

I matured early. In sixth grade I was 5'6" and 120 pounds. When I set a new school record of 5.9 seconds for the 50-yard dash the previous record holder—a boy—punched me in the stomach. I had good abs, so it didn't hurt.

In junior high, I set a record in the standing long jump and competed in every sport I could. In high school, I was a cheerleader for two years and participated in track, swimming, gymnastics, and badminton. As a junior I set a conference 50-yard freestyle swimming record and competed in the national championships.

My last year in high school, I concentrated on track, setting school records in the shot put, 100-yard hurdles, 220-yard dash, high jump, long jump, and as part of the relay teams. I won an academic-athletic scholarship to the University of Wisconsin-Madison, a Big Ten school.

Water to Weights

My first year in college I tried swimming and gymnastics, but at 5'8" and 145 pounds I wasn't built for vaulting. I was also getting waterlogged. I decided to concentrate on track and field.

I had never heard of the pentathlon, but my coaches knew all about it. They also knew I'd be perfect for it. Before I knew it, I was competing in the high jump, long jump, 100-meter dash, shot put and half mile. My favorite event was the shot put.

As a freshman I won the conference title in the pentathlon, setting a Big Ten point record. I went on to the nationals. I thought I would just be a small fish in a big pond, but I found myself in third place at the end

Competing in the long jump as a sophomore in a Big 10 track meet.

of the first day of competition. I started to get really nervous. On the second day, in the final event (the half mile run), I blew it. I was so nervous I started to hyperventilate and halfway around the track, I passed out!

I guess I have a thing for passing out. I continued competing in track and field, winning the Big Ten title on three separate occasions. In my junior year, I met Jeff Everson. My life was about to change.

He Tarzan, Me Jane

Jeff Everson was unlike anyone I'd met before. It wasn't just his physique, although at 6'3" and 250 pounds of big, blond muscle, he was unusual! No, his personality made him stand out for me. He was a National Collegiate Weightlifting Champion who could lift 425 pounds over his head, but he wasn't aggressive or pushy. Matter of fact, he was shy and witty. He set up weightlifting and conditioning programs for many athletes.

Me? I hated lifting weights. I know now I

disliked it because my coach had us lift after practice when I was dead tired. And then we had to do all these boring lifts like step-ups on a bench with a bar across our shoulders, dumbbell side bends, and jump squats. Ick!

One day, Jeff asked why I wasted time doing such nonsensical things when I should be doing regular Squats, power cleans, bench presses, and other lifts. I listened and tried what he had to offer.

I found out I was naturally strong. In my sixth heavy session of deadlifting, I lifted 310 pounds three times. I squatted 210 pounds eight times. I could bench press my body weight seven times.

Early in my senior year of college, I started losing interest in track. My old leg injury was bothering me. I decided to skip track and try badminton. I made it up to third woman on the squad. Our first woman was National Champion! I slowed up on my power training and concentrated on finishing my degree in interior design.

In March 1980, Jeff approached me about entering a bodybuilding contest. "Body-building? What's that?" Back then, women competitors spent time debating whether they should or should not wear high heels when they posed. When a reporter asked me what I thought, I said, "I never ran the

Here I'm trying my hand at a gymnastics vault.

My running background gave me a great foundation for leg development.

hurdles wearing high heels, so I won't pose in them either."

Jeff assured me that I would do well even if I didn't have much time to train. I had a good degree of muscularity from my sports and power training already. I had about one month to prepare. I dieted some, but spent most of my time perfecting a posing routine.

I BEGIN COMPETING

Eighty-two women entered the first annual Ms. Mid-America contest in Milwaukee, including yours truly. I trained off about seven pounds for the contest. Unfortunately, little of it was fat. Mostly I lost muscle and water. I didn't really know what I was doing. Thankfully, neither did any of the other competitors. I weighed 135 pounds. They called me a heavyweight. Believe me, I had never been called a heavyweight in anything I'd done before. Oh, well. By the end of the flexing I found myself the winner of the heavyweight class and doing final battle with someone named Tina Plakinger, the lightweight champion.

I managed to win the overall title. For those of you who know bodybuilding, Tina went on to win the Ms. America title, too, and to become a professional bodybuilder like me. We have competed against each other since then, but we still have the fondest memories of our first battle—without high heels!

A couple of months later, Jeff and I entered the first National Couples Championships. We finished third behind winners John Brown and Shelley Gruwell and runners-up John Kemper and Carla Dunlap. All of these people went on to be great champions. I don't think we looked much like bodybuilders. Jeff weighed 245 pounds and I, 142 pounds for this show. We weren't showing much definition or complete development yet.

In early 1981, before my blood clot, I was winning show after show. I won the Ms. Midwest and Central USA Championships. Then we won the National Couples. For most of my shows in 1980–81, I weighed around 138 pounds.

In 1982, I won the East Coast Championship. Again, I was known as that heavyweight from the Midwest. While I won the 11 heavies, Gema Wheeler won the overall title. Jeff also won the men's heavyweights. My biggest victory in 1982 came in July, when Jeff and I got married!

I tried for the American title in 1982 and finished fifth. Ahead of me were Carla Dunlap, Deborah Diana, Lori Bowen and Dr. Lynne Pirie. I was in good shape at 142 pounds. Several judges approached me after the show and told me I'd win this title within two years. I didn't really believe them, but turns out they were right.

A couple of months after this show, Jeff and I won the Northern Hemisphere Couples title in New York. I won the women's

Practicing our posing routine for one of our first couples competitions in 1980.

open division held in conjunction with the Men's Nationals won by Lee Haney.

In 1983, Jeff and I set our sights on one more couples title, the USA Championships held in Las Vegas. I didn't even enter the open women's division because I wanted to concentrate my efforts on the one show. We defeated a strong contingent and won unanimously. Jeff had a good weekend and also won the Men's USA Invitational Title.

The American Women's Championships were in Denver. I hoped to finish in the top three. I blew it though. Two months before the show I tore my back muscles doing deadlifts. For a long time I couldn't do anything. When I stopped training I let my nerves get to me, which just made things worse. I lost weight. I tried all kinds of therapies to heal the muscles including heat, ice, massage, and even zylocaine-cortisone. Nothing helped.

Finally, about two weeks before the contest it started to come around. Then I tried to get tanned too quickly and burned myself in a sunbed. I was a hopeless mess with skin peeling off every which way. In those days the fact that you should be 100% to compete didn't register. Although Jeff cautioned me about entering, I wouldn't listen and went in anyway. Big mistake. I finished

eighth. Although I did okay in the symmetry and proportion areas I fell in the muscularity section. I thought I was lucky to finish where I did, even though, incredibly, some people told me they thought I was better than Lori Bowen of Texas, who won the contest. I wasn't too upset, though. I knew the torn muscles were my downfall and there would be other contests.

The Battle of New Orleans

Nineteen eighty-three was a year of transition for Jeff and me. After the Denver debacle, I entered another national championship in San Jose that was held with the Men's Nationals. I had some time to train this time and moved up to second place. Again, several judges and fans told me I was on my way to bigger things.

Meanwhile, Jeff was being courted by Joe Weider to come west and work for him as a writer for *Muscle & Fitness* magazine. Jeff was in the middle of finishing work for his

doctorate in physical education. In late 1983 he and Joe came to terms, but in January 1984 we were taking Horace Greeley's advice to go west. California, here we come!

We decided that I should *not* take employment immediately in interior design. Instead, I decided I wanted to pursue a career as a full-time bodybuilder. By not working right away, I'd finally get all the time I wanted to train. Believe me, I made use of it.

For all of 1984, I concentrated on training my weak body parts. Before I left the Midwest, I visited my former doctors. They all felt that I could start heavy leg training again. They were satisfied that squatting would not damage my left leg.

I set my sights on the 1984 Nationals in New Orleans. I started training twice each day six times a week. I worked my legs so hard I thought they'd drop off. Because of neglect, my thighs were literally waiting to explode. They grew like dandelions. My hamstrings ballooned out, just like they were in my old track days. My thighs thickened and my body fat melted away. Most important of all, my head was really into training.

When the Nationals came I was ready. I weighed in at 145 pounds. Other than for my third Ms. Olympia victory, which came later, this was the best condition that I've ever been in. My main competition was veteran Diana Dennis. Diana and I had waged a few battles before. She was one competitor who always prepared well. She was always in shape (it's no different today—Diana finished third in the 1985 Ms. Olympia).

New Orleans was memorable because the judges opted for a somewhat less muscular look and instead put more emphasis on muscle proportion and symmetry. I won the show posing to the theme song from television's "St. Elsewhere." Jeff picked the music and every time I hear it I'm back on stage in New Orleans!

Winning the Nationals was the culmination of six years of direct bodybuilding training. I can't say it was an overriding goal of mine, though. As long as I can remember, my only real goal in bodybuild-

One of my first solo victories. Watch out world here I come!

© Trix Rosen

ing was just to do as well as I could and become as good as my potential would allow.

On To Montreal

Because Jeff and I have always shared the philosophy that it's better to train longer and harder rather than to try to diet your way to a winning physique, I felt I still had a fighting chance for the 1984 Ms. Olympia coming up in six weeks.

I felt that, should I enter, I would be under no pressure. No one expects a newcomer to walk right in and win the biggest professional show on her first attempt. I continued to eat and train as before. In fact, I tried to eat even more since I knew the tendency would be to lose weight because I was on the verge of overtraining, trying to prepare for two major shows in such a short time.

In hindsight, I was about 90% as good as my Nationals condition. I weighed 148 pounds, two pounds too much. The competition was extremely good, even better than

in 1983. Rachel McLish was at her all-time best and looked excellent. Fellow professional Mary Roberts was also in her best-ever shape.

I thought my symmetry and proportion were better than Rachel's and Mary's, and hoped that would make up for my lack of stage experience and any weak muscle areas I had. At the end of the first two rounds, I held a slim two-point lead over Rachel, with Mary third.

The final posing round proved decisive. I used the same routine that I won with in the Nationals. The judges liked it and I got all first places! Personally, I liked both Mary's and Rachel's routines, too, but I emerged on top. Wow, what a year! Winning both the National and the Ms. Olympia certainly put me on cloud nine.

Defending My Title

For much of 1985, Jeff and I were on the road. We traveled around so much I thought about switching careers and becoming a

Posing for the judges during my first Ms. Olympia victory in 1984.

stewardess. Even so, I continued to train hard, hoping to defend my title at Madison Square Garden the next November.

Two months before the show we stopped traveling. I had trained like a demon to get in my best possible shape. I'm now at the point in my career where I can't (and won't) enter any show unless I'm in optimum shape. When the big day came I weighed in at 146.5 pounds, in the best shape of my career.

I knew I would get strong challenges from Mary Roberts, Diana Dennis and several European women. In my eyes, Mary Roberts had the best muscle density and Diana was the most defined competitor. I hoped that I could out-balance them! Evidently, the judges again felt I had the best combination of muscularity, proportion, symmetry and posing because I won again.

To me, winning a second time was even more rewarding than my first victory. I proved myself as a pro, that I could train and travel at the same time and stand with the best women in the world. I was fortunate enough to win in 1986 too, my third victory.

I know the next few years will see women's bodybuilding become accepted as a major sport. One of the major reasons for this is because of women like Diana Dennis and Mary Roberts. Both are over 36 years old! When women around the world find out how bodybuilding can keep you in such fantastic, sexy shape at nearly 40 years of age, do you think anyone is going to keep them away from it? Not a chance!

Bodybuilding is such a positive force that it will not and cannot be impeded. In just eight years, since its inception in 1979, women's bodybuilding has grown tremendously. Already, major television networks and sponsors are bidding for the rights to women's bodybuilding shows. Soon you'll see it as a mainstream sport.

And for me, what of the future? I go with the wind. You never can tell. I may retire from active competition and move on to bodybuilding promotion. I might also train for the Olympic discus-throwing team. Or, I just may keep on trying to win the Ms. Olympia title. Whatever I do, you can be sure that I've enjoyed bodybuilding and that I will never abandon my roots. I want to continue making bodybuilding women's sport of the future. It's in my blood, and don't forget, my blood's bionic.

3
BODYBUILDING BASICS

Beginning any exercise program can be confusing. You have to know where you are going. Ask yourself *why* you want to train? Ask yourself *what* your goals are, what you hope and expect to accomplish with exercise. Your answers dictate your training program.

ALL EXERCISE IS NOT EQUAL

In George Orwell's *Animal Farm*, all the barnyard animals were equal, but some were more equal than others. (Orwell's barnyard was probably the *only* place where being a pig was admirable.) Any reasonable exercise program is good, but some exercise programs are better than others, depending upon your goals.

If you desire fresh air and a leisurely, recreational pursuit with moderate skills, golf might be your game plan. Should you be fortunate enough *not* to get angry every time you hook one off into a neighboring fairway, golf can be an excellent stress reliever, too.

If you want to lose weight and improve your heart and lungs, rowing, walking, running, and swimming might be your ticket. What about pure strength and power? Try Olympic weightlifting and powerlifting. For better flexibility, maybe a martial arts program is best. Martial arts is also the way to go for self-defense. If someone keeps kicking sand in your face or constantly intimidates you, karate will do more to protect you than anything Charles Atlas ever dreamed up!

Bodybuilding is *the* exercise system for firming your body, building sexy curves, losing or gaining weight—depending on your needs and achieving vitality, fitness, and a special radiance. You can also build quality muscle. Hopefully, some of you will go on to compete in bodybuilding.

Aerobics and Anaerobics

Exercise is divided into two broad categories, based on the energy pathways contributing to the activity. There's a lot of overlap, but exercise is classified as either aerobic or anaerobic.

Aerobic means "with oxygen." Anaerobic means "without oxygen." With aerobic exercise, oxygen is required to provide energy for the activity. Aerobic exercise is sustained exercise, involving large muscle groups. Aerobic exercise conditions your heart and lungs and increases your ability to take in and deliver oxygen to your cells. Therefore, physiologists consider aerobics the more beneficial form of exercise. In terms of life expectancy, they are right. You don't die because your triceps fail; you die because your heart fails! But, all exercise conditions your heart to a certain extent.

Anaerobic exercise is intermittent, usu-ally of short, stop-and-start duration. An-aerobic exercise requires short bursts of strength and energy. Stored energy in your muscles and carbohydrates are the main sources of fuel. Most active sports are anaerobic.

Quite unfairly, too many physiologists dismiss anaerobic exercise in favor of aerobic exercise. The problem with this outdated thinking is that people have different goals and desires. Cardiovascular fitness, although it's a very important part of overall fitness, is only *one* component of fitness.

Other elements of fitness include muscle strength, power and endurance, flexibility, agility, speed, quality of life, and freedom from disease. My opinion is that both forms of exercise are necessary for the highest

Running up stadium bleachers helps to supershape my legs.

possible fitness levels. There *are* activities that combine aerobics and anaerobics. Bodybuilding is one of them! That's why it's so great for shaping up.

Bodybuilding: The Best Form of Conditioning

While competitive weightlifting is purely anaerobic, bodybuilding training is not. A good bodybuilding program, especially one where you either rest very little between sets or not at all, helps elevate your heart rate for enough time to get some aerobic training effects. You also use your muscles for intermittent contractions, which requires anaerobic metabolism.

Although I believe bodybuilding is the best overall exercise, it *does not* cause as great an increase in your body's ability to utilize and deliver oxygen as pure aerobic exercise does. This capacity, often called maximum oxygen uptake, is considered the single greatest measure of cardiovascular efficiency. Bodybuilding workouts raise your heart rate for a long time and this is important for conditioning.

However, while some of that increased heart rate is due to increased muscle demand for blood, some of it is due to reflex pressure responses and adrenal hormones that are released in your blood in response to muscle fatigue products. If you have ever been flying in a plane and the plane suddenly hits turbulence and you drop 500 feet, you get an instant hot, burning sensation in your stomach. This is from adrenal hormones. Before you know it, your heart is pounding wildly, beating three times as fast as normal!

Heart rate increases from jogging and other aerobic activities on the other hand, have nothing to do with adrenal hormones or reflex responses. This is probably why some scientific studies show oxygen uptake increases from aerobics activities but not as much from bodybuilding. Nevertheless, bodybuilding does condition your heart and is a brilliant conditioning form, capable of

Training with a vengeance just before my most recent Olympia win.

enhancing every aspect of fitness. Anyone who dismisses it is simply ignorant of the facts.

The Tortoise Beat the Hare

The best place to start anything is at the beginning (unless you're telling a joke in Japan where they translate by giving the punch line first!). To get maximum results from bodybuilding, you can't jump on your Soloflex and head off in all directions at once. There must be a method to your madness.

If you set out to be a good swimmer, you wouldn't start on Olympic champion Mark Spitz's program. If you did, you'd sink. Would you attempt some of Mary Lou Retton's gymnastic moves your first time on the uneven bars? I think you get the picture. If you are just starting bodybuilding, you need to use a beginning program, not an advanced program. Your program must take into account your lifestyle, job energy demands, other commitments and your goals. This is why a beginner uses a different program than an intermediate or advanced trainee. My number one rule is to go slow and steady. Remember, the tortoise beat the hare in the long run!

IT'S THE PRINCIPLE OF THE THING

Your body is really a well-oiled machine that does what it's told. When you stretch, you get more flexible. When you jog, your heart pumps better. When you bodybuild, you shape up and lose fat. As with any exercise program, you must follow specific principles to make continual progress.

There are six key principles governing bodybuilding success. The first is *progressive overload*. Why does a bodybuilder get bigger muscles than a construction worker? The construction worker uses his or her muscles just as often, if not more often, than a bodybuilder, yet they don't develop as well. A mail carrier walks more than a competitive racewalker, but likewise, never develops the racewalker's endurance, strength, or muscle development. Why? The reason is progressive overload.

Bodybuilders continually force themselves to work harder, either by handling heavier weights, working out more often, or doing more exercises or sets of exercises. A construction worker, though, works a fixed amount of time per day and handles a varied workload. Some days there's a light load, some days a heavy load and some days no load at all. Consequently, there's no progressive overload.

The second important principle is *specificity*. I talk a lot about goals and constructing workouts to meet those goals. Specificity is the key. Let's say you want to get strong. You must lift heavy weights to develop strength. On the other hand, to get an enduring muscle, you can't use heavy weights. Instead, you need to do a lot of repetitions and that means using lighter loads.

Your muscles will respond to the type of stress placed on them. You need heavy weights and low reps for strength. You need high reps and short rest periods for muscle endurance. Just as a boxer doesn't go bowling to improve his boxing ability, so a bodybuilder must do what will give her best results. In other words, use a specific program.

If you pressed a five-pound weight overhead everyday, you wouldn't build much muscle. Surprised? You shouldn't be. You must use heavy enough weights to shape up. The amount of weight you use, relative to your absolute maximum capability, is referred to as *training intensity*. No one knows for sure what intensity is best for muscle size. For strength, loads of 75%–95% of your maximum single repetition are best. But for muscle size? No one knows precisely but it's a good bet that the weight you use for 8–15 repetitions is about right. This is what most bodybuilders do. The important point is, you have to use enough weight to force yourself to work hard. Intensity is the single most important factor for muscle growth.

Though intensity is critical, what if you only did one set once a month even though you used as much weight as you could? You wouldn't get very far, would you? Not only do you have to work out hard, you have to do enough to grow. This is called *training volume*. Training volume refers to the number of sets you do. Usually, more sets are better, provided they are intense enough. But there is a limit! You can't just keep doing more and more sets or you will overtrain. It takes time and experience to learn just how many sets of each exercise, or for each body part, you can, and should, do. You also need to work out often enough. This is called *training frequency*.

Finally, to specialize on a muscle, to get it to grow fastest, you have to work it in relative isolation from other muscles. If you want your leg muscles to grow, you don't do neck bridges or sit-ups. You do squats. Although your muscles (all 600 of them) work together, you can isolate skeletal muscles fairly well. Isolation is a technique all bodybuilders use in individual exercise movements.

Adhering to these six basic principles—progressive overload, specificity, training intensity, training volume, frequency, and isolation—is critical for success.

FIRST CAME ADAM AND EVE, THEN THE BARBELL

Barbells and dumbbells are the bodybuilder's fruits of life. Free weights are the easiest and best way for a bodybuilder to reach her goals. Do not be afraid of them. Don't believe what you hear about free weights not being as safe as machines. It's just as easy to hurt yourself training incorrectly on a machine as it is with free weights. And, should a machine be in disrepair, it might be easier to injure yourself on the machine.

People argue a lot over which is better for a bodybuilder, machine training or free weights. I think this is a senseless argument. If both are available, why worry about it? Why not just use both? That's what I do.

Some people insist that machines are better for flexibility and slimming while barbells are better for muscle strength and size. Machines aren't better than free weights for flexibility. Likewise, as long as a machine is a good one, there's no reason at all why you can't build muscle size and strength from working on it.

There are a lot of great machines around. However, while the quality of barbells and dumbbells is constant, some machines are clearly much better than others. Because machines only allow you to exercise in a specific, fixed pattern, they don't put as severe a stress on your muscles. Obviously, you can't build a machine that will fit everyone perfectly.

Dumbbells and barbells go wherever you push them. Machines do not. Some machines cost $4,000 and you can do only one or two exercises on them. Unless you have

money to burn and own a big house, machines like the $4,000 one are a bit impractical for home use. Barbells and dumbbells are inexpensive and versatile. This is their main advantage over machines. You are also required to balance free weights as you lift them. You don't have to worry about this on machines. If you have to balance the weights, your muscles work harder and you gain more control over them. This helps you develop them better and faster.

As I said, machines aren't as practical for home use. In a gym, you should take advantage of all the equipment available. Most commercial gyms have machines that isolate muscles. Machines for leg extensions, leg curls, hack squat machines, Smith machines, long pulley row machines, and lat pulldown machines are great. Don't listen to those who tell you to use only machines or only free weights. They don't know what they are talking about.

Once you decide where you're going to

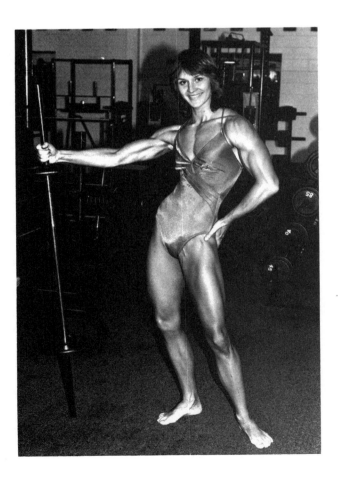

train (it really doesn't matter *where* or *when* you train, only that you *do* train), you next have to decide what type of workout is best for you. This is where I come in.

START SLOW AND BE ORGANIZED

Imagine how you'd feel if you wanted to learn to fly, signed up for lessons and the first day your instructor put you behind the controls of a Boeing 747 and said, "Okay, kid, this is it. We're going to start with a solo flight." Pretty stupid, huh? Well, don't laugh, some bodybuilders without any experience at all expect to follow my advanced program. That's not the way to do it.

At first, you need to follow a simple, organized basic plan. Your routine should consist of just a few exercises, each designed to work a specific muscle area. Generally, a beginner (anyone with less than six months' bodybuilding experience) should train three alternate days a week with the weights. If you are on a mixed program for shaping up, you can do aerobics on your "rest" days.

Learning technique is critical. In bodybuilding, we refer to "getting the feel" of a movement. This means you learn the techniques of the exercises, techniques that best isolate and "pump" your muscles. This produces growth.

You should always keep your program simple when beginning. If you exceed your capabilities, you won't make progress. So don't overdo it, and allow appropriate time for rest. Recovery of your energy supplies is essential for growth. This recovery process can be increased with time. This is how your body adapts to progressively higher stress levels. You can't afford to push too hard too fast.

There are two things you must remember right from the start: Technique is always king, and warming up is something you never forget to do! Study the pictures and exercise descriptions that accompany the charts in each of the following chapters.

During your first few training sessions, don't use any weight at all so you can familiarize yourself with all the movements without worrying about what weights you are using.

Always start out with a few stretching exercises and light calisthenic movements (arm circles, jumping jacks, etc.) to limber up. This helps lubricate your joints, increases the temperature of your blood, and increases your circulation through a stepped-up heart rate. Following good warm-up procedures will help you avoid the injury demon throughout your bodybuilding years.

Beginners Anonymous

Why do I say that anyone with less than six months' experience is a beginner? Well, I'll admit that this is only an arbitrary standard. Some people bodybuild for years but train like they started yesterday! Then again, some fast gainers take to weights like catsup to a french fry!

But the average person takes around six months before she has learned all the basic nuances of exercise technique. It also takes a good six months of basic work to measure your responses to training. Are you the type who can take a lot of work and still want more, or do you fatigue fairly fast? Remember, bodybuilding is about progressive adaptation and you need time to adapt to higher workloads. For most people six months seems about right for the initial stages of adaptation.

As mentioned, beginners should train three days a week. I recommend one to three exercises for each body part. For instance, beginners might do curls for biceps, but Squats, Leg Extensions, and Leg Curls for their thighs. You should do at least two, but never more than three sets of any one exercise to start with. To organize your training, you'll learn to divide your body into parts such as chest, shoulders, back, arms, legs, and abdominals. Later on, you'll subdivide your body parts. Legs are broken down into quads, hamstrings and calves. Arms will be broken into biceps and triceps.

Back may be divided into upper and lower back. It's important to understand this terminology.

What about other important terminology? I just mentioned the word *sets*. A set is a series of movements of an exercise. These movements are called *repetitions*. For instance, if you lift a weight in the two-hands curl 10 times, rest, and do 10 more, you've just done two sets of 10 repetitions each in the curl. That's bodybuilding jargon at its most basic level.

Other terminology will follow. Beginners should start exercising with body parts nearer the center of their body and work outward. This is because your biggest muscle groups are closer to the center of your body and you should expend more energy on big muscle groups because they have the most growth potential. Obviously, if you spend an hour doing chest pressing exercises, you'll get better overall growth than from spending an hour on wrist exercises. The same is true with your legs.

You'll get more benefit from an hour of squatting than you would from an hour of ankle exercises. The exception to this is when your goal is to shape up a weak or out-of-shape area. For instance, flabby thighs or abdominals. These are two areas women really need to watch and you may want to set up a program just to go after those areas. (Later on you'll see that I've devoted separate chapters to these problem areas).

"How much weight should I use for my exercises? How many sets should I do? How many repetitions should I do? Should I explode when I lift or go slow? How should I breathe? Do I need a spotter on every exercise?" These are all good questions I hear a lot.

Let's start with breathing. Some experts insist that you should inhale any time you *lift* the weight and exhale during the down or relaxation phase. Others suggest that you exhale during the lifting phase. *This is better.* I recommend that you exhale as you make the lift and inhale as you lower the weights. *Do not hold your breath.* This is where problems develop. Holding your breath at the same time you exert yourself can increase intrathoracic pressure (Valsalva Phenomenon) and can cause decreased blood flow to your head, which leads to dizziness. So, don't hold your breath! If you can't learn to breathe out or exhale as you lift the weight and inhale as you lower your weights, then just breathe naturally. Don't even think about it. Make things easier on yourself.

You can't do too many sets before you're ready for them. That's why one to three sets is best for novices. If you have six basic body parts to train and you do an average of two exercises for each, that's 12 exercises. Doing two to three sets of each means you do 24–36 sets in one workout. Believe me, that's plenty for a beginner! Later on, as you progress and adapt, you'll sometimes do 20–30 sets for one body part alone! But not yet.

Making Muscles Grow

What about repetitions? Most bodybuilders like to vary their reps from 8–15. I like to go up to 20 reps (and sometimes even higher). Low reps and heavy weights build strength, but not necessarily muscle size. Weightlifters are strong, but they don't have big muscles like a bodybuilder. No one knows exactly what makes a muscle grow. It's a certainty that individual muscle fibers hypertrophy (grow larger) and they may also replicate themselves (hyperplasia). The individual myofibrils or actual muscle filaments thicken, but other areas of the muscle grow, too. Perhaps the demands of oxygen delivery and nutrient exchange involved with higher reps (the 8–20 range) causes better overall growth.

Just as we know that mid-range reps with heavy weights are best for growth, we also know that really high reps don't contribute to growth, but they do give you muscle endurance and some vascularity (increased capillary and venous networks).

As a general rule, stick with 8–15 repetitions. This will provide you with the best combination of muscle tone, shape, strength, size, and proportion. When you do

partner or partners, they can provide occasional support. Whether you train with a partner or not, you still need to follow the rules of the game—good technique and safety first.

About training partners: some bodybuilders like them (I do) and some do not (Jeff does not). A partner provides support, encouragement, and motivation (at least she should!). A good training partner is like an extra spoke in the wheel. If you do train with a partner (I recommend that you do), select one who is serious and will stick to triceps and biceps instead of dragging you into her personal life.

Atlas Held the World on His Shoulders

Some bodybuilders pretend they're Atlas and get carried away trying to constantly lift heavy weights. Though heavy weights are important, so is technique! If you isolate the muscle group you are working and train strictly, you won't have to use so much weight, but you'll still get the same growth. Remember, you are a bodybuilder, not a competitive weightlifter. It doesn't matter how much you lift. It matters *how* you lift.

It's really impossible for anyone to tell you how much weight to lift in each exercise since strength is relative. Once you've learned correct technique and after you've warmed up with light weights, you should strive to use as much weight as you can on all your sets for the required repetitions. For example, if the set requires 10–15 repetitions, your training weight should not be so heavy that you fail after seven repetitions. Nor should it be so light, that you can power out beyond 16 or 17 repetitions.

Experience will teach you what weights are best for you. I can't. If you still need a guide, begin each body-centered exercise with approximately one-third your body weight. If you weigh 120 pounds, try to use around 40 pounds (or less) when starting out. Then, gradually increase. Write your workouts down in a training log so you can chart your progress.

your repetitions, *do not* explode and try to move your weights fast. You don't get any points for finishing your set faster. Actually, most bodybuilders use a steady, constant exercise cadence. This gives you control and through control, you develop. Moving deliberately under control also helps you avoid injuries. Some people claim that moving the weights fast develops more muscle fibers. There is little scientific support for this.

There will be a few occasions where spotters, people who can catch the weight should you be unable to finish a repetition, are necessary. The Squat and the Bench Press are two such lifts. Otherwise, you don't need spotters. If you train with a

Oh, My Aching Muscles!

If you have never trained before and you start out going gangbusters, you probably won't be able to move for a week! Even well-conditioned athletes get sore muscles if they do something they are not accustomed to. No one knows for sure what causes sore muscles although it's probably a combination of small, minute muscle tears and increased fluids, like lactic acid and other connective tissue enzymes, in the muscles after exercise. Not only do these products put pressure on small nerve endings, causing pain, but the lactic acid causes the blood to be more acidic and this irritates nerves.

Muscle soreness is indicative of hard work. It is not bad, just uncomfortable. If you start slow, though, and break in gradually, you will not get this soreness. Your body does accommodate to exercise. Your metabolism gets more efficient and you get used to the lactic acid. You no longer experience those minute tears. If you train regularly, muscle soreness will be a thing of the past!

The Rules of the Game So Far

Here's a short review of the nuts and bolts I've discussed so far.

1. Use both free weights and machines.
2. Always stretch and warm up before training.
3. Emphasize safety and technique at all times.
4. Follow a systematic, organized program.
5. Start slowly and build up gradually.
6. Use partners if you want. Use spotters when necessary.
7. Beginners should train with weights three alternating days of the week.
8. Do a maximum of three exercises per body part.
9. Do between one to three sets of each exercise.
10. Do between 8–15 repetitions on each set.
11. Other than on your initial warm-up sets, use the heaviest weight you can for the required reps.
12. Stay on a beginning program for at least six months.
13. Progressive overload, training volume, training intensity, frequency, specificity, and isolation are bodybuilding principles to live by.

SIX MONTHS AND BEYOND: INTERMEDIATE BODYBUILDING

There comes a time when every bodybuilder needs a change. Most serious bodybuilders want to go as far as they can. However, it's really impossible to add any more to your present daily workout. Everyone has limits of time and energy. Adding work on each of these days would be counterproductive.

It's time for a split system of training. What's a split system? On a split system, you do not train your whole body on one day. Instead, you train different body parts on different days. The original concept of a split system was to train your upper body one day and your lower body the next. Today, however, bodybuilders have expanded this concept. Here are a few ways a lot of intermediate bodybuilders use the split system.

SPLIT SYSTEM ONE

Monday: chest, shoulders, back, and arms
Tuesday: rest
Wednesday: quadriceps, hamstrings, calves, and abdominals
Thursday: chest, shoulders, back, and arms
Friday: rest
Saturday: quadriceps, hamstrings, calves, and abdominals
Sunday: rest

SPLIT SYSTEM TWO

Monday: chest, shoulders, back, and arms
Tuesday: quadriceps, hamstrings, calves, and abdominals
Wednesday: rest
Thursday: chest, shoulders, back, and arms
Friday: quadriceps, hamstrings, calves, and abdominals
Saturday and Sunday: rest

Some bodybuilders like to keep their weekends free, but I recommend you train your upper body on Monday and Thursday and your lower body on Wednesday and Saturday when beginning your intermediate phase. This gives you more rest during the week. Later on you can switch to the more advanced systems.

If you want to train by body parts, but not upper body/lower body, here are some more recommendations, but these are harder programs.

SPLIT SYSTEM THREE

Monday: chest, shoulders, and triceps
Tuesday: quadriceps, hamstrings, calves, and
   abdominals
Wednesday: back and biceps
Thursday: rest
Then repeat the four-day cycle.

Another way to train on the split system is as follows:

SPLIT SYSTEM FOUR

Monday: chest, shoulders, back, and
   abdominals
Tuesday: quadriceps, hamstrings, biceps, tri-
   ceps, and abdominals
Wednesday: rest
Then repeat the three-day cycle.

On one system, you work each body part twice a week. On the other, you work some of your body parts three times a week. Both systems are generally more difficult than the upper body/lower body approach. However, I give you this option because I believe in hard work. Some intermediates can handle this; some can't.

What are some other differences between the beginner and the intermediate? I'll hit on this theme even more in coming chapters, but switching over to a split system allows you the time and energy to do more exercises and more sets for each body part. This produces better gains.

As a beginner you did one to three sets per exercise and two or three exercises per body part. On an intermediate split system you usually do three or four exercises per body part and three or four sets of each exercise. You do more work. A beginner might do four to six sets for her chest. An intermediate would do up to a dozen sets.

The rules stay the same. You use the same principles as before and you still do a wide range of repetitions, usually between 8–15 (I go higher, up to 8–20).

I already discussed the advantage of doing between 8–15 repetitions. This builds size, shape, and definition. Intermediates use a few different techniques incorporating this system. We call this holistic training because it ensures that all aspects of your muscles develop.

How do I use a holistic system? I start with a light weight and do 20–25 repetitions. Then I *pyramid* my weights up and progressively decrease my repetitions. I do this for the next couple of sets, but I never do fewer than 8 reps (in fact, I usually stay at 10). Then I *reverse pyramid* and lower the weights and increase my reps back up. I don't do this with every exercise, though. On a lot of my sets I stay very conventional and just do my basic sets with a fixed number of reps and a fixed weight. I always use the heaviest weights I can unless I'm tired or sore.

Super and Giant Sets

Besides differences in the number of exercises and sets that intermediates do compared to beginning bodybuilders, they also use more advanced training techniques. Supersets and giant sets are two of these methods.

With a superset you do one exercise for one body part immediately followed by another set of an exercise for a different body part. Usually the body parts you superset are opposite or antagonistic to each other. Every muscle has an antagonist.

When you curl, your biceps contract. Its antagonist, the triceps, relaxes. Many bodybuilders superset their biceps and triceps or quadriceps and hamstrings, feeling that they get additional development from this. Personally, I don't do a lot of supersets, but on occasion, I do.

A giant set is a series of four or more exercises where you do one set of each without any rest in between them. (Note: A tri-set is three exercises grouped together. I will explain how I use tri-sets in my chapter on Sexy Shoulders.) When you have completed one set of all four or more exercises in a nonstop fashion, you've completed one giant set. I think giant sets are appropriate for training abdominals and for slimming and toning stubborn thighs. Some bodybuilders also use them for slow-developing body parts, such as deltoids (shoulders).

You Gotta Want It!

Another distinction between intermediates or advanced bodybuilders and the beginner is their motivation levels and ability to concentrate. Bodybuilders are determined athletes. Those who push on through beginning and intermediate levels to become competitive bodybuilders are extremely motivated individuals.

Lots of times I hear people say they want to improve the way they look, but they just can't get motivated to do something about it. Well, if they can't get motivated, then it's obvious they don't want to improve themselves very much! Bodybuilding is really self-motivating because your improved shape and physical looks provide enough rewards.

Usually, at the start of any exercise plan, your motivation is high. Your goals are fresh and you are anxious to see what you can do. Sometimes, progress is not as fast as you would like and you lose motivation. In bodybuilding, you must be patient and you must keep negative thoughts out of your mind. One way to stay motivated is to train with an equally enthusiastic, serious partner. Another way is to change your routine (sets, reps, and exercises) around. This helps put boredom at bay.

Later on, when you read about my workouts, you'll see that on some exercises I set goals or standards that I try to achieve. I don't do this in many exercises, just a few. This constant goal-striving keeps me motivated. This is one advantage to training in a gym with partners. There's more friendly competition.

Still, when it comes down to that set and rep, you must be able to shut the outside world out and lose yourself for a moment in your exercise. Every great bodybuilder knows how to concentrate on the task at hand to develop maximum muscle quality. Visualize your muscles. Visualize your goals, the way you want to look. Believe and you shall achieve!

It's All in the Genes

The social and biological sciences have collided for years. Arguments over which is more important toward shaping personality have raged on for centuries. I can tell you this—in bodybuilding, genetics is very important!

It is true that within a small deviation, everyone has the same basic physiology. However, differences in metabolic rate, bone size, inherited shapes, and tendencies to store fat affect the rate of development and the overall results achieved from bodybuilding. Everyone can improve tremendously. There's little doubt of that. But not everyone has the potential to win Ms. Olympia. There should be equally little doubt of that.

Don't be deterred if you don't make the gains that you see others making. Everything is relative. Some people can gain muscle and lose fat easier. Some women have faster metabolisms, better structure, and maybe even slightly higher levels of male-type hormones.

Remember, gains are relative to yourself. Only worry about Ms. You! Be your own judge, measure yourself by your own goals and capabilities. If you stick to the good nutritional practices and training programs outlined in my book, you'll succeed in the end.

Sometimes Less is Better

Some people are "hard gainers." They are better off staying at the beginner level or staying with an intermediate program, never moving to a so-called advanced plan. Usually, people who are doing everything right, like getting enough rest and sleep, eating well, and freeing themselves of stress in their lives, but who are not making gains, are most likely overtraining in their workouts. They are trying to handle too much of a load—maybe too much weight, training too often, or doing too many sets and exercises. For some reason, they just cannot handle it. Almost always, when people ask my advice because they are not making good gains, they'll increase and spurt ahead again after I have them cut *back* their programs.

Dwindling enthusiasm, motivation, and concentration are the cardinal signs of overtraining. If you stop looking forward to your training, something's not right. If your mind drifts when you are in the middle of your workout, something's not right. If there's no pressing emotional or personal problem that you might be dealing with at the time, then it's a good bet overtraining is the problem!

There are other signs of overtraining, too. General fatigue and lethargy indicate an overtrained state (providing you are getting enough sleep and eating right). Night restlessness signifies overtraining. So does an increased pulse, loss of appetite, headaches, loss of strength, weight loss, sore muscles and an aching feeling in your joints. I guess it sort of sounds like the flu, doesn't it? These are the same symptoms, only with overtraining you don't feel sick and the signs are not always clear.

My advice to people who experience these symptoms as well as losing motivation, is to cut back and see what happens. Most beginners and intermediates are overly enthusiastic and try to do too much. This is why I

stress that you stay on the beginner's program for at least six months and the intermediate program for another six months after that, before you try more! If you don't seem to be making the muscular growth gains you want and you always feel tired and dragged out, cut back on your sets and exercises and see what happens. Chances are you'll get enthusiastic and start progressing again. Sometimes less is better!

ADVANCED TRAINING

What differentiates an intermediate from an advanced bodybuilder? An advanced bodybuilder knows the capabilities of her body to adapt to varying training volumes and intensities. An advanced bodybuilder finds a way to make her workouts harder and more productive. Generally, advanced people have more desire, more knowledge, more time to train, and a better capacity for adaptation. There isn't really much difference in terms of the structure of their workouts. They still train once a day (some train twice a day), and they rotate their body parts in the same way an intermediate-level bodybuilder does.

However, there are differences. Most advanced bodybuilders train on either a three-day-on one-day-off system or a two-day-on one-day-off system. Although most train just once a day, their workouts may take three hours to finish. Some bodybuilders (including yours truly) train twice a day.

Increased Volume and Intensity

The big difference between advanced and an intermediate trainee is an enhanced volume and training intensity. An advanced woman trains harder and more often. Usually, advanced women do 4–6 exercises per body part and between 4–6 sets of each exercise. This means she could do anywhere from 16–36 sets per body part! I would guess that most advanced bodybuilders average 20 sets for larger muscle groups (thighs, chest, back) and around 10–15 sets for smaller areas. I like to do 25–30 sets for most body parts, but have done up to 60 sets for my legs in one day! Observation tells me that advanced subjects still prefer 8–15 repetitions for most exercises.

Advanced women who train once a day usually use a three-day-on one-day-off system. This method appears to be almost universally popular with competitive bodybuilders around the world. Advanced women group the body parts differently. Two of the major ways are as follows:

ADVANCED SPLIT ROUTINE ONE

Monday: chest and shoulder
Tuesday: back and arms
Wednesday: legs and abdominals
Thursday: rest
Friday: start cycle over.

ADVANCED SPLIT ROUTINE TWO

Monday: chest and back
Tuesday: legs and abdominals
Wednesday: shoulders and arms
Thursday: rest

Of course, there are variations to these methods. Besides the increased sets and exercises and greatly increased training time, advanced bodybuilders occasionally use tougher training techniques. These include negatives, forced repetitions, double-split training, giant sets, tri-sets, and supersets.

Double-Split Training

With a double-split training system you train twice a day, once in the morning, and once much later in the day. As you might surmise, this is a very difficult and time-consuming way to train, but a lot of advanced bodybuilders are, or want to be professionals. Not only are they willing to put this time in, *they have to!*

There is another increase in intensity and volume with a double-split. The bodybuilder now has even more time to spend on each individual body part so she does more sets (and sometimes more exercises) once again. A double-split plan requires energy and time and also motivation and a high level of elite adaptation. Some professionals *never* reach this level of adaptation and find that they overtrain if they try it. Here's the way many advanced bodybuilders use a double-split.

ADVANCED DOUBLE SPLIT ROUTINE

Monday A.M.: chest and abdominals
Monday P.M.: back
Tuesday A.M.: quadriceps and abdominals
Tuesday P.M.: hamstrings, calves, and low
    back
Wednesday A.M.: shoulders and abdominals
Wednesday P.M.: biceps and triceps
Thursday: rest
Friday: start cycle over.

Many bodybuilders work their calves and abdominals three or four times a week and "throw them in" at the end of either their morning or evening session, wherever they feel their time merits it. This is another distinction of advanced bodybuilders. They understand how their bodies respond to exercise so well that they can freewheel their training and be very creative according to their individual needs. Joe Weider named this *instinctive training.*

I will elaborate much more throughout this book on how to group body part exercises together and why you should or should not do things certain ways. I also will constantly hit home on the differences among beginner, intermediate, and advanced bodybuilding programs.

It's What Goes Up That Counts

Bodybuilding used to be like the old saying, "There are only two things that always go up in life, your age and taxes." Bodybuilders used to just be concerned with how much weight they could lift up. Now they also worry about how much weight they can lower. At least, some bodybuilders do.

Negative training is a very advanced, intense method of training. Two or more people lift a very heavy weight up for you and then you resist it as gravity pulls it back into position. Thus, you work your muscles in a negative or eccentric contraction. This is also called *retro-gravity training.*

You are very strong in negative work (this is due to high intramuscular friction, not because you innervate or use more muscles) and consequently you have to use over 100% of what you can lift one time in a positive contraction. This is dangerous and very intense, hard work. Most bodybuilders *do not* do negatives because it is very easy to overtrain on them. However, some bodybuilders use them.

The way most bodybuilders use negatives is at the end of a set of positive contractions. For instance, let's say you've just finished a set of 15 reps in the leg extensions. You are all pooped out on positive work so now you have someone lift the end of the leg apparatus up and then they push down on it while you resist its descent back to the starting position. They lift it up again and you repeat your negative contraction. This method seems to work for those who enjoy torture!

I don't use negatives. I haven't seen any studies convincing me that they are better than very hard positive contractions. I also think negatives can lead to overtraining and injury, so I leave them alone. However, should you want to try them, they are grueling and you need a willing partner or partners to lift the weight up for you. That might be the most difficult thing about negatives—finding someone to lift the weights up for you in the first place!

Forced repetitions is another advanced technique. As you end your normal set and can no longer do the repetitions on your own, your training partner assists you to finish a couple more reps. Thus, you "force" them out. The theory behind forced repetitions is that you still have the ability to generate some muscle force in some parts of the exercise range of motion. Assistance at bad leverage points allows you to finish a few more repetitions and therefore, you should get better results.

The theory sounds fine and a lot of bodybuilders do use forced reps. Some have, or claim to have, made very good gains from forced reps. I suspect many have. However, this is a very stressful form of training and must be used judiciously. I'll be honest—I don't do many forced reps. In fact, the only exercise where I ever use forced reps is on Scott curls for my biceps. I do believe that too much emphasis on forced reps and negative training can lead to overtraining, injuries, and early burn out. You are essentially trying to *exceed* the momentary muscular capacity and fatigue of your body. That is *always* dangerous, so be careful!

No Pain, No Gain

I'm sure most of you have heard or read this statement somewhere. But what does it mean? After all, how could pain be good for making gains? I don't like this phrase because it implies that something bad, something injurious, is worthwhile. I also don't like the expression because ignorant people, outside of bodybuilding, have misinterpreted its meaning!

When you do a very hard set of exercises and just barely make all your reps (in other words, you really have to push it at the end), fatigue products of muscle contraction build up in your blood and cause an uncomfortable ache in your muscles. Hitting a peak, at the end of your set, this ache doesn't last long. After a couple of seconds the discomfort is gone. Bodybuilders know that if you never experience any of this discomfort, you're not working hard enough. That's where the expression came from, but doctors and others have interpreted this expression to mean the pain caused by injury. Saying "No injury, no gain" doesn't make much sense! Well, who doesn't agree with this?

This exercise discomfort is not bad and

The mind in bodybuilding is so important. Here I'm performing a Concentration Curl for peak bicep development.

does not indicate injury. All it means is that you are working hard and you will make gains because of it! So play it again, Sam!

TIME IS ON MY MIND: REST INTERVALS

How long should you rest between sets? I recommend that a beginner rest 90–120 seconds between sets. This is probably a little longer than you may have read elsewhere, but I think beginners need more time to recover between sets. Beginners are just learning the fine nuances of technique. If you are fatigued, skill breaks down and technique is harder to learn. Longer rest periods will prevent this.

Since most beginners are trying to gain muscle size, they also need to rest more between sets. More rest means better recovery. Better recovery means you'll get stronger, capable of handling heavy weights for your reps. Heavy weights generally (but not always) mean bigger muscles!

The exception to my rest interval suggestion would be for someone who is training to increase cardiovascular fitness or get rid of excess body fat. In these cases, the less rest you take between sets, the better!

As you progress in bodybuilding, decrease your rest intervals between sets. As an intermediate or advanced bodybuilder, the quality of your physique is most important. At that stage, you shouldn't rest any more than 60–90 seconds between sets. If you train with a serious partner, this is just about the time it'll take her to finish her set.

Competitive bodybuilders, in preparation for a contest, sometimes rest 30 seconds or less between sets (especially if they are supersetting, tri-setting, or giant setting). My overall advice is that you not be a slave to the clock. After a while you get an intuitive feel of how long to rest between sets. All you need is enough time for momentary muscular recovery and then you plow through another set. You want to keep a good pump in your muscles because that's what makes muscles grow!

INJURIES

Needless to say, as with any sport, you must avoid injuries at all costs. Injuries delay progress. Injuries almost *always* take place when you exceed your capacity. This can be an acute episode where you try too much, or it can be a case of pushing beyond your limits over a long time, which leads to chronic micro-trauma of the muscle and degenerative conditions within your joints or tendon attachments. Both cases represent the worst of overtraining.

To prevent serious muscle strain or pulls, train intelligently. Always warm up and use strict technique. Never cheat a weight up! If you do, you're liable to cheat yourself into a hospital bed.

Do not try to handle weights beyond your capacity. Make sure you take the required days of rest when your routine calls for them. If you do suffer a slight strain or pull, rest it until it's ready to go again. Don't rush an injury; if you hurt it again as you come back, it could develop into a serious chronic injury. Start back slowly and when you do, always warm up really well and use high reps and moderate weights to start with.

Most injuries in bodybuilding are not serious, but if you are ever performing an exercise and you hear a loud snap or pop and an immediate loss of power, immobilize your injury, apply ice, and consult a physician immediately. Don't dillydally. Get to a doctor right away.

Besides warming up and using good technique, I advise wearing a weight-training belt for a lot of exercises, especially the squat, deadlift, and overhead pressing movements. A weight belt will equalize the

I stretch religiously before each workout. It's imperative for injury-free training.

outward pressure of your abdominal contents when you exert yourself. It also gives you a tight, support feeling that helps you learn technique better, especially in the squat.

I'm convinced that a bodybuilder, training correctly doesn't ever have to suffer an injury. Train intelligently and you've got it made in the shade!

AGE IS A MATTER OF MIND, AND IF YOU DON'T MIND, IT DOESN'T MATTER!

I'm *not* in favor of specific bodybuilding exercises for very young boys and girls. General sports participation is better at young ages. Diverse athletic pursuits will give a youngster a broad base to expand on and give her a choice of future activities to play and possibly compete in.

There's no age rule as to when you can start bodybuilding. You can make gains at any age, but I think your best gains come from working out between the ages of 15 and 35. A second tier of good gains can be experienced by those in the 35–50 age group and then another level of gains occur if you start (in good health and with a physician's directions) after age 50.

Several champion women bodybuilders are in their forties. Notables include Dr. Lynne Pirie, Mary Roberts, Diana Dennis, and Kay Baxter. I've seen several women over 50 start bodybuilding and make outstanding progress. Don't ever ask me if it's too late to start because it never is!

Of course, as you age, your recuperative powers slow. Your body tissue is less resilient and your muscles need longer rest periods between workouts. Older bodybuilders need to do fewer sets and exercises because of their decreased recovery factor. If you are in good health with normal blood pressure, there is no reason why you can't benefit from a good bodybuilding program. The fact of the matter is, I believe older individuals *need* bodybuilding *more* than youngsters because of their natural loss of muscle with age!

What about the young bodybuilder? Girls do mature earlier than boys (one of our many superior traits) and can actually take harder workouts earlier than boys. However, I don't think anything is gained by going on a very intense workout program in your early teens. Mine is only an opinion, but this is a time in your life for experiencing a lot of activities and you shouldn't lock yourself up in a gym all the time. However, there is no reason that you can't get on a beginning routine and bodybuild in your early and mid-teens and then progress so that you are going full tilt by your late teens and early twenties. Just keep in mind that no one becomes a National or World Champion with less than 5–7 years of hard work and a little genetics in her favor.

4
WHY DIET IS A DIRTY WORD

The fact that you're reading this book means you've made an important decision in your life toward improving yourself physically. Toning, shaping up, and bodybuilding for fitness is a goal we all should have! The next logical step is to learn how to eat correctly.

The very first thing to understand, unless you are so overweight that it's causing medical problems, is that the conventional concept of dieting has got to go! Dieting implies deprivation. Deprivation is a negative reinforcement. You have to give up something and that's bad. Instead, you need to adopt a nutritional plan that satiates you psychologically and physically. You must view nutrition from a "What will my foods do for me today?" plan rather than a "What do I have to give up today?" plan.

For many unfortunate individuals, eating the wrong foods (as well as overeating any food), is related to their frame of mind. Many people overeat when they are depressed and bored. Then again, some go to the other extreme and practice anorexia (self-induced starvation) or bulimia (binging and purging food) when they are unable to control their emotions or accept their personal image. These people need psychological help. I'm not a psychologist and I won't pretend to be. All I know is that bodybuilding improves your self-image and makes you more confident. It's an excellent way to work off personal tension. It also allows you to eat more of those "bad" foods that everyone seems to like!

But why do I suggest that diet is a dirty word? Don't most doctors tell Americans that 50% of us should be on diets? They do, and most of them are wrong because they know nothing about correct dieting. And, dieting as we know it now is almost always wrong!

Statistics reveal that of the countless millions of people who go on diets, only a whopping two percent actually lose weight permanently! Something's wrong. If the dieting concept was valid to begin with and if it worked, why do people always go *off* their diets?

41

YO-YOS ARE FOR KIDS!

Conventional dieting is like a chemical yo-yo. People who are always dieting go up and down, back and forth, stop and start. All of this could be avoided if they'd just learn to eat right. Did you know that dieting without exercise can actually make you fatter than when you started? Reduced-calorie diets that are not correctly balanced can cause biochemical changes in your body that can make you fatter than you were before!

What usually happens when you go on a diet? If you stick with it, you usually lose a few quick pounds the first couple of weeks. Almost all of this weight loss, though, is water, and it comes back as soon as you start eating and drinking normally again. All of a sudden any further weight loss slows to a crawl. Why?

MAINTAINING THE STATUS QUO

Your body perceives any reduction in calories from what it is used to as a form of starvation. Responding to this threat, your body slows itself down, to better save nutrients important to your existence. Your metabolic processes slow to maintain the status quo. In effect, your body likes fat and will do whatever it needs to keep it. What in evolutionary terms is quite an amazing set of metabolic life-saving adjustments turns out to be pretty depressing for the dieter! All of which makes it more difficult to shape and tone up at the dinner table.

Scientists are learning more and more about human metabolism (metabolism is the sum processes of ingesting nutrients and utilizing them for all our basic body functions). Your body is efficient at saving calories. Like animals that hibernate and live off their stored fat by slowing their metabolisms, humans do much the same on long, protracted diets.

I've known 140-pound women on 800–1,000 calorie-a-day diets who do not lose weight, even if they exercise! I suppose a few of them might be eating more calories than they say, but I believe a lot of sincere, honest women fall into this category and simply do not know what to do to shape up. Fact is, most of them have been on calorie-reduced diets so long that their metabolisms have all but stopped!

Scientists know that we have the capacity to slow our metabolisms down by over 50%. Humans have an amazing capacity for survival. Recall stories of little children who have been submerged for up to an hour in freezing water after falling through the ice and still have survived. Their metabolism slowed way, way down and mobilized everything possible to save blood sugar for their brain. Likewise, someone who diets for extended periods might slow her metabolism to the point where, if she once needed 1,800 calories from food to maintain her weight, she now needs only 900 calories to maintain!

What are calories and how do they relate to metabolism? A calorie is a unit of heat. Whenever you expend energy you create heat. This heat can come from one of two sources, either through the food we eat or from existing body stores.

Every activity you do requires some heat, some calories. Your basal metabolism is the amount of calories you would burn if you were to lie still, doing nothing but breathing for 24 hours. People with fast metabolisms have high basal or natural metabolic rates. These people, it seems, can eat as much as they want of almost anything and never get fat.

Added to your basal calorie requirements are the calorie costs of your physical and mental activities. As you sit reading this, you are burning calories (hopefully you're breathing). If you are reading this while riding a stationary bike, you are burning up more calories because your muscles are working.

Conventional dieting is based on the premise of give and take. If you take more from your body than you give it you'll lose weight. If you do not provide your body with the calories it needs through food, then presumably you will take those needed calories from your body and thus, lose weight. The formula is correct, but it's the way your body takes those calories that's misunderstood. For a person who wants to slim and tone or especially for those who want to add muscle mass, understanding the pitfalls of normal dieting is crucial.

Saving Grace

Your body's saving grace is that it protects you so well. It signals you when something is wrong. Have you ever noticed how air-brained you get if you go without food for a couple of days? Your brain is signaling you that it needs nutrients. The same spaced-out effect happens to bodybuilders on low-carbohydrate diets. Santa Monica, California, is full of bodybuilders who wandered out into the streets without looking and now have casts on their lower legs from being bumped by cars! All because of low carbohydrate diets that weren't doing them a bit of good anyway!

Besides saving glucose (sugar) for the brain, your body also likes to store fat. Fat gives support, energy, and protection to your body. I've met many athletes and non-athletes who can't get rid of fat from certain places. People who want to shape and tone up still have jiggly rears. Bodybuilders who want sharper definition can't seem to get it in their frontal thighs.

Genetic patterns determine fat distribution. Women tend to store fat in their hips, buttocks, triceps, thighs, and waistlines. Often, diets leave these women with large lower bodies and skinny upper bodies. Or, worse yet, dieting doesn't do anything at all! Most of this is due to misconceptions about dieting and exercising.

Tricking Ms. Metabolism

Every individual is a victim of her genetics. Everyone has a predetermined pattern of fat storage. Everyone has a unique metabolic rate. Scientists tell us that people hold their weight within a closely guarded range. The tendency for an adult's weight to stay fixed is called the biological setpoint.

Evidently, your hypothalamus gland, which determines or controls basic drives, like thirst and appetite, "sets" your body functions (including metabolism) to maintain a specific weight, a specific status quo. When you attempt to deviate from this pattern, as when taking in fewer calories to lose weight, your body responds by slowing itself to save calories. However, there are ways to adjust your setpoint. Exercise and correct dieting are two of them.

How do the type of foods you eat affect your setpoint weight and metabolism? All food is composed of fats, protein, carbohydrates, water, fiber, vitamins, and minerals. Three of those elements—protein, carbohydrates, and fats—provide energy. This energy comes in two basic forms, glucose and fatty acids. Glucose (sugar) is produced through the metabolism of proteins and carbohydrates. Glucose that is stored in your muscles and liver is called glycogen. Fatty acids are produced through the metabolism of fats.

Fats. There are three kinds of fatty acids (fats for short). These are saturated, monounsaturated, and polyunsaturated. Every dietary fat is made up of a combination of these three. Saturated fats are essentially solid at room temperature (like a stick of butter). Most mono- and polyunsaturates are liquid at room temperature (like cooking oils). All three types of fat provide energy.

There are three essential fatty acids which the body needs, but can't produce on its own. These are linoleic, arachidonic, and linolenic acids. They are unsaturated fatty acids necessary for growth and healthy blood, veins, nerves, and arteries. Fats are necessary in your body to transport fat-soluble vitamins (co-factors in body reactions). Vitamins A, D, E, and K are your fat-soluble vitamins. Fat converts carotene to Vitamin A and surrounds and protects your organs. When one gram of fat is metabolized, it yields over nine calories!

Carbohydrates. Carbohydrates are combinations of various sugars. Some sugars, such as those in honey, digest very easily.

Other sugars are complex in nature. This includes carbohydrates found in rice, pasta, whole grains, and cereals. Complex sugars are called long-chain carbohydrates. When you do activity of short duration and high intensity, you use carbohydrates for fuel. When carbohydrates are metabolized for energy, they yield four calories per gram.

Protein. Proteins are made up of combinations of amino acids. Some amino acids can be produced by your body, but others, called essential amino acids, must be taken in through your food. Complete proteins contain all eight essential amino acids. To ensure the proper protein structure for your body, you need all the essential amino acids. Animal food sources (eggs, meat, fish, and milk) contain all amino acids necessary for proper protein synthesis. Vegetables and grains do not contain all these essential amino acids. However, by combining different vegetable sources (a grain and a legume, for example), you will get the necessary amino acids for growth.

Protein is necessary for growth and maintenance of body tissues, including hair, skin, muscles, blood vessels, and all your internal organs. Protein is generally not used as an energy source, but like carbohydrates, supplies four calories per every gram that is metabolized.

Vitamins and Minerals. Minerals and vitamins are critical for healthy metabolism. Minerals are inorganic compounds such as copper, calcium, iron, phosphorus, magnesium, and sodium that maintain cellular function. Minerals make up bones and teeth, and are essential components of soft tissue and nerve cells. Minerals can be obtained only through your diet.

Vitamins are organic substances that work as co-factors in metabolic reactions. They are essential for growth and normal development, but they *do not* contribute energy to reactions. Vitamins are complex chemicals that are effective in very minute quantities. Vitamins A, D, and K can be formed in your body (although "precursors" may be needed) while all other vitamins, including Vitamins C, B, and E, must be obtained from your food.

FOOD AND YOUR METABOLISM

You've probably heard that too much fat, especially saturated fats, contribute to heart disease and stroke by raising cholesterol levels in your blood. Cholesterol is a type of fat that exists normally in the body, being produced by the liver. It has essential body functions. However, when you overproduce or take in too much cholesterol in your food it can be deposited on the walls of your blood vessels. This can lead to premature hardening of your arteries, heart attack, and possibly stroke, should part of the cholesterol plaque dislodge and travel into your brain circulation.

Too much fat, then, is a medical problem as well as a cosmetic one. Fats are especially deadly to a woman who wants to shape or tone up and even more so should she decide to become a serious bodybuilder. New research suggests that fat calories are stored selectively in your hips, thighs, and buttocks—whereas calories from carbohydrates are not! It seems we are back to Orwell's *Animal Farm.* All calories are not equal, especially fat calories!

People who eat high-fat foods gain weight more readily than those who eat high-protein or carbohydrate foods, *even if the total caloric intakes are equal*! It has always been thought that you turn *any* excess calorie into fat. Well now, as it turns out, it's much harder to turn excess protein and carbohydrates into fat!

Dietary fat is already fat. Carbohydrates and protein are not. Therefore, from a metabolic standpoint, it's much harder to convert carbs and proteins to fat. In fact, assuming your kidneys are healthy, almost all excess protein is eliminated from your body. Carbohydrates are not easily stored either and are generally used for energy.

Carbohydrates and fats are your two main energy sources. Fats provide energy for daily maintenance and also contribute to sustained activities of an endurance nature (jogging for 60 minutes, for instance). Carbohydrates provide energy for short bursts of activity, such as cleaning the house in an absolute frenzy before your guests arrive. Converting dietary fats and carbohydrates to usable energy is not an equal process.

Converting 100 grams of carbohydrates into fat consumes about 25 calories from your body. Converting dietary fat (100 grams) into body fat costs about 3–5 calories! Consequently, you can eat more carbs without getting fat. Fats yield more than twice as many calories per gram and they are also easier to convert to body fat from an energy cost standpoint.

Animal studies reveal the same things. Pigs fed calorically equal diets of corn (which contains fatty oils) and wheat (which doesn't), gain weight on the corn diet, but do not on the wheat diet! Rats fed equal calories, but one group in the form of a high-fat diet and the other in the form of a high-carbohydrate diet, do not gain weight equally. In fact, the rats on the high-fat diet gain weight, while the high-carb fed rats do not.

Your body loves to store fat, but not carbohydrates. No one gets fat on fruit, no matter how many apples they eat. Because carbohydrates cannot be converted to fat without a greater energy cost, they have the capability of changing your biological set-point. It's believed by many doctors that carbohydrates have a thermic effect. This means that they create more heat to metabolize. This fact supports evidence that they can reset your setpoint. People wishing to "diet" or shape up or tone up or gain muscle definition or lose fat or just obtain better heart and blood vessel health should drastically cut their dietary fats and start replacing them with long-chain, complex carbohydrates.

Fat Cells: 'Til Death Do Us Part

Sometimes it seems that fat is like taxes; it'll be around forever. If you measure the number of fat cells on two hard-training, competitive bodybuilders, both of whom have trained for the same time with the same intensity and nutrition, you'd still find that one will have more fat cells than the other.

By the end of puberty you have all the fat cells you're ever going to have (at least that's the present scientific thought, although lately, some scientists say that fat cells can increase at any time). Fat cells can shrink or expand, but they never go away unless you have them surgically removed.

If you go on the wrong type of diet and don't accompany it with exercise, your fat calls may shrink, but so might your muscles. Skeletal muscle accounts for around 40% of your body weight and between 35%–45% of your energy consumption. That means the more muscle you have, the more calories you burn. Muscle is metabolically active, requiring calories just to maintain itself. Fat is inert and does not have its own calorie requirement (except perhaps "brown fat," which some scientists now suspect may have its own metabolic requirements).

If you diet and lose muscle mass, your calorie needs are diminished. This means that if you go off your diet and gain weight back, but don't gain the weight as muscle but as fat, you'll suddenly need fewer calories than before you started your diet. You are worse off than before!

Furthermore, fat cells shrink, but they stay around waiting for a chance to refill again. It's critical then that you don't eat a lot of fat when you are young and develop too many fat cells. Be born of lean parents, too, if you can help it, since the tendency to be fat *is* inherited!

Because fat cells merely shrink and dietary fat fills them up faster than any other food, you should stop eating almost all fat in lieu of carbs and make sure you exercise your muscles. When you do follow a low-calorie diet, any fat that you lose usually is subcutaneous instead of intramuscular fat. This fat comes back *faster*. Secondly, when your fat cells shrink, they release an enzyme called lipase which (hold on to your seats) actually *encourages* fat storage. Dieting becomes a deadly circle. You start dieting and your fat cells shrink. You release enzymes that make it easier for the cells to fill back up! Meanwhile, your body tries to maintain its status quo so it slows itself down. This creates a need for fewer calories than before. Your body further attempts to save fat, so it starts using available muscle for energy. Dieting thus causes a loss of muscle, which again slows your metabolism. Almost every factor says that deprivation *dieting* is bad.

GENETIC AND OTHER FACTORS

There's more to this sordid story. Some unfortunate people lack critical cell enzymes responsible for mineral balance across the cell membranes. Much of our basal metabolism is devoted to the maintenance of cell membrane potentials. People with low cellular transport enzymes have naturally low basal metabolic rates and this makes it easier for them to gain weight.

On the other side of the coin, some people have more brown fat (fat is either yellow, white, or brown) which is highly specialized for heat production. The higher your percentage of brown fat, the more efficiently you burn calories. Evidently, the amount of brown fat you have is determined genetically.

Besides not eating enough carbohydrates, people also make the mistake of consuming all their calories in one meal. They save up all day long, so they can eat as much as they want at their nightly meal. However, experiments with humans and animals show that eating once a day mobilizes enzymes which store fat better so you retain more fat from your food. Athletes, or anyone conscious of her weight, should eat balanced meals spread throughout the day rather than stuffing themselves at one meal.

What About Sugar?

Bodybuilders have typically shunned sugar, but is all sugar so bad? After all, carbohydrates are simply combinations of various sugars. Sugar in and of itself is not bad. It's just that refined sugars contain no nutrients (other than calories) and disrupt your insulin production and increase your appetite. Refined sugars get into your bloodstream quickly. A sugar like table sugar (sucrose) causes your pancreas to increase its output of insulin immediately. Insulin is a hormone that transports sugar across your cell walls from your blood. High levels of insulin *slows* the breakdown of body fat. And, sugar disrupts your appetite. Even artificial sweeteners stimulate your appetite. They act the same as natural sugar.

Refined sugars then are not nutritious and are detrimental to controlling your body fat and weight. Of course, a sweet now and then isn't going to kill you. Believe me, I've had my share! If you train hard, you transport a lot of the sugar out of your blood so you don't need to produce so much insulin. Excess is what makes the goose plump!

No one, bodybuilder or anyone trying to lose weight or shape up, should ever stop eating carbohydrates. In fact, everyone should eat *more* complex carbohydrates. People who try to stop eating carbs usually last about 7–10 days before their brains signal (command is a better word) them to eat carbohydrates. The delicate chemical balance in your brain is disrupted on low-carb diets. People who follow these plans simply end up binging on carbs about every 10 days. Because carbs hold water chemically, your weight goes up and down from water imbalances. Carbohydrates are superior to fat and you should never try to cut them out of your nutritional plan. Bodybuilders, because of their high energy demands, need much more carbohydrate than the average person.

The Good, the Bad, and the Ugly

Fat is ugly. Refined sugars are bad and complex carbohydrates are good. Why, if basic sugar is bad, aren't all carbohydrates composed of sugars bad? Well, driving 20 miles an hour in a 25-mile-an-hour zone isn't bad, but driving 50 miles an hour is. By the same token eating an excessive amount of carbohydrates that rapidly spill sugar into your blood disrupts normal body functions, while eating complex carbohydrates, which empty sugar into your blood slowly, actually assists normal body functions.

The bad, refined sugars are found in candy, chocolate, pie, cakes, cookies, sweet rolls, brownies, ice cream, and all those delectable gooey things we call desserts! Good carbs are found in fruits, potatoes, lentils, beans, peas, pasta, breads, cereals, whole grains, legumes, fresh fruit juices, and rice.

So maybe you don't like the taste of some of that stuff. I have no control over the fact that society has conditioned our taste buds to crave sugar and fat. You'll just have to decondition them. Concentrate on the life-prolonging, good qualities of complex carbohydrates. They provide less than half the fat-producing calories of dietary fat. They aren't easily stored for energy. Instead, they are "thermic" foods that create heat, speeding up your metabolism and creating unlimited energy. Complex carbs provide bulk, too, which is healthy for our intestines. Why, there's even some evidence that diets high in vegetables and fruits help prevent cancer of the colon, heart disease, and high blood pressure. Think about these things and before you know it, these foods will start tasting a *whole lot better.*

Protein Power for Bodybuilders

You can't convince me, after I train for six hours in a day, that I have the same protein requirements as a sedentary woman with 25% body fat. Any nutritionists who still cling to this outdated thought probably drive a Model T, too. Most of these people are moderately well-read, but have never set foot in a gym.

Protein requirements for bodybuilders have been debated for years. While it is most assuredly true that most sedentary people eat too much protein, it's also true that hard-training bodybuilders need more protein than the average person. This does

As you get more advanced in your training, nutrition plays a far greater role.

not mean that bodybuilders need to take supplemental protein. It only means that you should make sure you get enough complete protein from your regular food. If you are a vegetarian or don't have a taste for protein foods, then you should consider supplements.

Researchers at Kent State University recently conducted studies that indicate that the nutritional world has been understating athletes' protein needs. They found that when dietary protein falls below 12% of your total calorie intake, you start using your own muscles to provide the necessary protein. Vegetarians and pregnant women who exercise may fall into the same cannibalistic trap.

The Food and Nutrition Board of the National Academy of Sciences, is responsible for establishing the RDA (recommended daily allowance). The RDA is an upgrade of the original minimum daily requirements. The RDA "allows" for individual absorption and genetic differences, as well as any drop off in the protein quality. Still, they figure that a sedentary 120-pound woman needs only 43 grams of protein a day and a sedentary 180-pound man needs 66 grams of protein a day.

Since protein doesn't contribute significantly to energy, why does a man need more protein? More muscle mass perhaps? The researchers at Kent State say yes. If you exercise and are trying to build muscles you need extra protein.

I believe a bodybuilder should eat between .50 to .70 grams of complete protein for every pound of body weight. If you weigh 120 pounds, you should eat between 60–84 grams of protein a day. This will be plenty. Eating extra protein beyond this range just taxes your kidneys.

Carbs and Fat Needs

Bodybuilders need a lot of carbohydrates. So do people who earnestly want to shape and tone while losing extra fat. Both groups need all the energy they can muster. Therefore, eat unlimited amounts of long-chained carbohydrates, but cut way back on your fats, particularly saturated fats. Carbohydrates help you assimilate your protein, too. Carbohydrates are a regular jack-of-all-trades! You don't need to count grams of carbohydrates. It's a waste of time. Your energy level will inform you when you are not getting enough.

What about fats? You do need the three essential fats, but that's about it. You need enough fat for normal body functions like the transport of fat-soluble vitamins. Fatty foods may help the ultra-endurance athlete, like the marathon runner. However, eating fats is self-defeating. While it increases your body stores for energy, the extra weight you add works as a mechanical drag, decreasing your efficiency.

I recommend the following percentages for anyone who wants to shape up with bodybuilding: 20%–25% of your daily caloric intake should come from complete proteins and 65%–70% should come from natural carbohydrates, especially complex carbs. Finally, 10%–15% should come from fats, most of it unsaturated fats. Generally, if you eat a lot of fresh fruits and vegetables, you'll get all the fiber, vitamins and minerals you need to.

IMPATIENCE IS NOT A VIRTUE

You say you can't wait to lose weight in your quest to shape and tone up? Well, if you insist on rushing into a diet, incorporate what I've told you so far. Match your caloric intake with your normal needs. Make the bulk of your food carbohydrates. Start exercising, emphasizing your muscles. Do not try to lose more than one pound per week.

Lower your consumption of fats enough to trim off 250 calories a day. Just cut your nightly chunk of meat in half and drop one large glass of whole milk from one of your meals. Or, if you don't eat or drink this, cut out fat somewhere else. Maybe that creamy salad dressing should go. Then add 250 calories of exercise each day (see the Appendix to see how many calories are burned with various activities).

You'll now have a net withdrawal of 500 calories a day or 3,500 calories a week from your fat bank. That is equivalent to one pound. For a while, you'll lose one pound a week. As your metabolism slows itself, don't cut your calories any more! Instead, increase your complex carbohydrates and decrease your fats even more and exercise more. You'll achieve the results you want slowly and surely. Being impatient is not a virtue. Slow and steady is!

DON'T SABOTAGE YOURSELF WITH UNDERCOVER CALORIES

Figuring out how many calories you are eating can be very tricky. Some foods considered high in calories actually aren't. For instance, popcorn popped in oil contains just 40 calories per cup. Keep it unbuttered. If you air pop it, it's ridiculously low in calories and is a good, filling snack. A slice of bread is usually 70 calories. You could eat 30 slices through the day and still be under your daily caloric need. One-half cup of rice gives you only 80 calories, a bowl of oatmeal around 130 calories. Potatoes vary, but an eight-ounce one is usually about 150–160 calories. Think you'd be full if you ate 14 eight-ounce potatoes in a day? What about 20 apples? A good-sized apple provides 100 calories.

On the other hand, typical "good" foods often are higher in fats and calories than you'd probably guess. The popular snack, trail mix packs a whopping 1,200 calories in a cup! Ouch! Polyunsaturated vegetable oil, although there is some indication it works to lower cholesterol, contains 120 calories per tablespoon! Finally, that healthy bowl of granola you love for breakfast can saddle you with up to 600 calories per cup. If you have a large bowl for breakfast, you've just about had it for your daily caloric intake. There's a lot of fat in granola.

Let's take a look at the bodybuilder's friend, Mr. Salad Bar. (With friends like this, who needs enemies?) Do you like croutons? Ten croutons give you close to 100 calories. If you take two tablespoons of sunflower seeds, chalk up 102 calories. Now you know why sunflowers are the biggest flower in the garden! Let's say you scoop up on cheddar cheese. Two lousy ounces (which to a cheese-lover is just a smidgeon) saturates you with 224 calories. Creamy cottage cheese supplies 240 calories per cup and 40% of that is fat! Forget the mayonnaise. At 100 calories in a tablespoon, you should gladly skip it.

This is not to say everything on the "low-calorie" salad bar is bad. Ten mushrooms provide only 25 calories. A cup of alfalfa sprouts yields 50 calories. Twelve skinny carrot sticks supply 30 calories. And, of course, you can eat a whole head of lettuce with nary a moment's worry about its calories.

Finally, tread cautiously with your salad dressings. Most people average about 5–8 tablespoons per large salad. That'll give you anywhere from 300–600 extra calories from most dressings (Ranch, creamy Italian, Thousand Island, French or blue cheese). However, if you use eight tablespoons of low-cal dressing, you'll get 160 calories—or less.

Be cautious with what you eat. Don't sabotage yourself before you start.

IF YOU CAN'T TRAIN OR DIET FAT AWAY, "SUCK" IT AWAY!

Sometimes, through such things as repeated pregnancies or abdominal surgery, your abdominal muscles suffer irreversible damage, your abdominal contents sag, and fat accumulates. Pockets of fat can form and are totally resistant to diet and/or exercise. In these severe cases, skilled surgeons can remove some of this fat in a process called liposuction.

The candidate for this surgery is a person who is unable to lose fat through correct nutrition and exercise and who has pockets of fat in specific areas. It is not a procedure for general obesity. And, it has complications and doesn't perform miracles.

Basically, the surgeon inserts a tube called a cannula through a one-quarter inch incision in a high-fat area. The tube is attached to a high-suction vacuum that literally sucks out fat. You can remove only a small amount of fat at a time, but chances are your appearance will significantly improve!

Backstage with a good friend and fan, Mary Lou Retton.

DON'T DIET, DO WHAT I DO

Bodybuilders don't need liposuction. That's only for people with a real fat problem in very limited, specific areas. Bodybuilders don't need to worry about excess fat, either. We need to eat for maximum muscularity and shape.

Rather than limit my food, I believe in working harder and burning more calories. I'm a carbohydrate freak. As long as I can remember, I've been a bread nut. It's my favorite food. When I go out to eat, the bread I'm served beforehand is often more important than any entree.

Breads without spreads are okay. Adding butter, peanut butter, mayo, or jellies gives you useless calories. Even when I eat pizza I scrape off the toppings and eat the crust. I suppose it's odd, but my instinctively high-carbohydrate and low-fat diet keeps me lean year round.

I eat a lot of rice, oatmeal, shredded wheat, breads (all types), salads, fruit, tuna fish, baked potatoes, egg whites, vegetables, turkey, fish, and de-skinned chicken. I don't eat red meat (it's loaded with fat) or french fries. I care not for any alcohol. I do have a weakness for hot dogs, catsup, Milky Way bars, and an occasional morning bun. Generally, though, my fat content is low. Usually, if I want a snack, it'll be bagels or popcorn. I never use salt or eat salty foods, either.

I eat a lot of small meals throughout the day and I drink quarts of bottled water and diet soda. I'm trying to wean myself of the sodas! Although I don't count grams or calories, I'd guess I take in 100–125 grams of protein and about 3,500 calories a day.

What about supplements? I don't like swallowing pills. I try to eat well so I don't need supplements. However, approximately three months before a contest, when I start watching what I eat, when I start heavy training two and sometimes three times a day, and when I get involved in this stressful situation, I start taking supplements. I take egg white protein powder, amino acids, especially lysine, calcium, iron, carnitine, inosine, Vitamin C, and a balanced multivitamin/mineral capsule. Carnitine helps release stored fatty acids from your liver for increased energy and inosine helps create ATP (adenosine triphosphate) in your cells. This increases your energy. Not everyone needs supplements. I suggest you experiment to see if various supplements help you.

THE FINAL FOOD REVIEW

1. Eat more complex carbohydrates.
2. Limit refined sugars.
3. Drink a lot of water.
4. Cut your fat intake drastically.
5. Eat enough complete protein, but don't overdose.
6. Always go on an exercise program if you diet.
7. Limit your salt and alcohol intake.
8. Don't go on conventional diets with severe calorie restrictions. Instead, increase your carbohydrate calories and decrease your fat calories.
9. Do both aerobics and anaerobics.
10. Eat frequent small meals rather than one or two large meals.
11. Of your daily calories, 20%–25% should be protein, 65%–70% complex carbohydrates and 10%–15% fats.
12. Never lose more than one pound a week.
13. Be patient and work hard!

5
SLIM THIGHS AND BUTTOCKS

Have you ever said to a friend, "I'd love to, but I can't eat ice cream. It goes right to my thighs!" Bodybuilders say it often. In fact, chances are many women have made this statement. Why does fat settle in the thighs?

Scientifically, it doesn't make much sense. If fat is metabolized evenly, why indeed do some women get heavy thighs but stay relatively slim everywhere else? Why, when some women go on diets, do they lose weight everywhere except from their thighs? And why do bodybuilders have such a hard time gaining definition in their thighs?

According to the laws of entropy, energy can neither be created nor destroyed. It can only be transferred from one form to another. To lose weight you must get rid of more calories than you take in. A calorie is a measure of heat. When you lose weight, you lose heat. So why can't women lose the heat from their thighs when they seem to do it everywhere else?

I've already explained that excess calories are stored as fat—especially if those calories come from fat! Because of metabolic, structural, and genetic differences, women store fat at different rates and in different places than men. If they overeat, men get big stomachs and love handles (that's what they call them, anyway). Women get flabby bottoms, hips, triceps, and thighs. Not only do women store excess fat in their thighs, but this fat seems impervious to removal even for bodybuilders! Even the strictest of diets do precious little. The old adage, "First on, last off," seems all too true. A lot of women who go on diets but don't exercise right, end up looking like pears with thin shoulders and heavy legs.

FAT BY ANY OTHER NAME . . .

Many women who are busy raising families (or involved in some other time-and-energy-consuming profession) lose touch with their physical condition. They forget about exercise and might be too busy feeding their families properly to feed themselves right.

What happens? Before they know it, presto chango, they're overweight, especially in the thighs. At the same time they find themselves lugging extra weight, they've lost the strength to do so as their lack of exercise has caused a rapid loss of muscle tone. Sometimes, the fat on the thighs and buttocks looks dimpled. Because of its peculiar appearance and its penchant for hanging around, it gets a special name, cellulite.

Fat by another name is still fat. And that's all cellulite is: fat. Forget theories that cellulite is a special fat surrounded and trapped by excess fluids and cellular toxins. Forget eclectic programs of bodywraps, weird massages, foreign creams, fancy lotions, and useless vibrating machines to attack cellulite. Viewed under a microscope, fat taken from a cellulite deposit is the same as fat taken from anywhere in the body. You have to treat it the same way as regular fat.

Why does cellulite look the way it does, then? With loss of muscle tone, connective tissue loses its support base. As fat accumulates, it causes your skin to lose elasticity. Everything droops and your thighs and buttocks look dimpled.

The only way to eliminate fat is through controlled exercise and diet. Losing fat and gaining muscle tone require a program that does three things: it must raise your overall calorie usage rate (called basal metabolism), specifically tone up your thigh muscles, and teach you to eat properly. Learning to eat the right foods is critical to your long-range success. Unfortunately, there are no miracle pills that magically burn calories. Nor are there any foods that take more calories to digest than they contain—the mythical "negative-calorie" foods.

The Buttocks

Your buttocks consist of the gluteus maximus, minimus, and medius. They cover the back and sides of your upper legs. Not only are these muscles the thickest in your body, but when you measure the force these muscles can generate proportional to the cross-sectional area of muscle fiber, your gluteus

maximus is the strongest muscle in your body!

Your butt muscles are active in just about every activity, whether it be standing, walking, jumping, lifting, biking, or running. These muscles are directly responsible for lifting your leg backward or straight out to the side. They also help rotate your legs outward. Activity is the only way to shape them up. If you sit around a lot, you'll develop a heavy layer of fat over your buttock muscles to serve a comfort and protective function. It's no secret that losing fat on your backside is very difficult.

In some fitness books, you'll see models performing all kinds of exotic-looking machine and pulley exercises, backward, forward and every which way, to shape up their buttocks. All this extra exercising is unnecessary if you do conventional exercises.

Take a look at the buttock muscles of competitive female race walkers, jumpers, sprinters, bikers, hikers, runners, and body-builders. Anyone who practices any of these activities on an intense, regular basis does not, and will not, have a saggy, unattractive butt!

When you do exercises such as Lying and Standing Leg Curls, Leg Presses, Squats, Hack Squats, Hyperextensions, Deadlifts, Smith Rack Squats and Lunges, you work your entire gluteal complex. Add aerobic activities, such as hill walking, biking, jogging and/or swimming, together with improved habits at the dinner table, and you'll effectively get rid of all excess buttock fat as well as building maximum muscle tone.

I'm confident that if you follow either my slim thigh exercise and diet plan or my leg building program, you'll "end" up with beautiful buttocks.

EXERCISE RIGHT!

As I've explained earlier, exercise of *any* kind raises your metabolic rate so you burn calories at rest. When you're actually exercising, you burn calories then, too. As for your thighs, unfortunately, you can't spot reduce fat (unless you know a skilled plastic surgeon). The idea that you can is a myth.

However, fat is released as heat at different rates from different areas of your body. This is how the spot-reduction myth was born. This is why you may lose some fat from your upper body *before* you start losing it from your thighs. Especially if the only form of exercise you do is aerobics.

Lest you think I have anything against aerobics, I don't. You need both aerobic and anaerobic exercise to confront a thunder thighs condition. Because aerobics involves large muscle groups and significantly increases your heart rate, it is very efficient for burning calories. It also requires fat for fuel. Therefore, walking, jogging, rope jumping, skipping, rebounding, swimming, stair climbing, stationary biking, regular road-biking, rowing, aerobics classes, and cross-country skiing must be a part of your strategy to vanquish thigh fat.

Aerobic activities are a good way to burn fat calories. More intense forms of exercise require carbohydrates. Aerobics, on a calorie-per-calorie basis, are better then anaerobics for weight loss. Elite cross-country skiers can burn 1,200 calories in an hour.

I'm prejudiced toward certain aerobic exercise. If you want to lose weight *and* tone up your thighs, then do aerobics that *stress* your thighs. Walking, stair climbing, and biking are best. I recommend fast walking for most people because it's easy to do without any kind of skill to learn. It's also easy to apply progression to walking plans.

Here's a simple plan to try. Start each session with five minutes of slow walking to warm up, and finish with five minutes of slow walking for a cool-down.

WEEK ONE

Walk one-half mile every day over flat terrain. Take about 12 minutes to go that distance.

WEEK TWO

Walk one mile every day over the same terrain in about 22 minutes.

WEEK THREE

Walk two miles a day over flat terrain in about 40 minutes.

WEEK FOUR

Walk two miles every day, but now include hills in your terrain. Take 45 minutes to go two miles.

WEEK FIVE AND ON

Gradually try to increase the time and distance you walk (as far as you can go in 60 minutes, going at least three miles) including a lot of hills in the terrain. This will continue to be an aerobic activity, but will also work your thigh muscles.

Fast walking over a hilly terrain, 60 minutes each day will provide a good aerobic workout. It'll also burn about 500 calories a day, or 3,500 calories every week. This means you could "walk off" one pound of fat each week.

Even though there are 3,500 calories burned off in one pound of fat, this does not mean you will lose 52 pounds of fat in a year. Theoretically, maybe, but practically it won't work this way. As I mentioned in an earlier section, your metabolism slows itself down when confronted with a continuous calorie demand or calorie deprivation. Therefore, you should periodically change the format of your walking plan and even switch to another aerobic activity.

I recommend stationary biking as a substitute for walking. You don't have to worry about dogs or the weather or worse. Jogging is too stressful and swimming takes a high degree of motor efficiency. If you pedal a bike for 60 minutes at a suitable intensity, you also can burn 500 calories. To keep boredom at bay, read the morning newspaper or watch your favorite television program as you ride to slimness.

The Right Exercise

Fast walking, swimming, skipping, rope jumping—all are good ways to slim thighs. However, there's a caveat. Aerobics alone are not enough! The very fact that they are not specific makes them less than perfect candidates for firming your thighs. You need bodybuilding for that.

Only bodybuilding has the capability to slim and tone your body. Walking or jogging doesn't significantly change your body shape and muscle tone. Bodybuilding will accomplish this, firming and slimming your thighs. You need both forms of exercise to reach your goal. There are no excuses for the serious slim-thigh seeker!

A 45-minute bodybuilding leg circuit is just the ticket. The best way to slim and tone your thighs is to group four bodybuilding exercises together and do one set of each exercise, one right after another. Famous bodybuilding trainer Joe Weider calls this a giant set. I recommend four groups of exercises done on four different days of the week. Here are the giant set sequences that work best:

Giant Set One
1. Squats
2. Lunges
3. Leg Extensions
4. Leg Curls

Giant Set Two
1. Leg Presses
2. Standing Calf Raises
3. Standing Leg Curls
4. Lunges

Giant Set Three
1. Hack Squats
2. Seated Calf Raises
3. Lunges
4. Lying Leg Curls

Giant Set Four
1. Leg Extensions
2. Lying Leg Curls
3. Leg Presses
4. Lunges

How does the giant set system work?

Just before starting, do a brief warm-up and stretching session. Do the first exercise 12–20 times (repetitions, or reps). Now you've completed a set of the first movement. Without rest, go directly to the second exercise and do 12–20 repetitions. Again without rest, proceed to the third exercise and do 12–20 repetitions. Finally, go right to the fourth exercise and do 12–20 repetitions.

You have just finished *one* giant set. After this you take a brief rest and then go through the whole thing again three more times!

All together, you do the giant set sequences four times for a total of 16 individual sets of four different exercises. Believe me, if four days a week of this doesn't firm up your flabby thighs, nothing will! Even competitive bodybuilders use this method.

A FIRST-DAY SAMPLE PROGRAM

Exercise	Sets	Reps
Giant Set One:		
Squats	1	12–20
Lunges	1	12–20
Leg Extensions	1	12–20
Leg Curls	1	12–20

Repeat Giant Set One three more times. Then do these basic bodybuilding exercises.

Bench Presses	2	10–15
Lat Machine Pulls	2	10–15
Shoulder Presses	2	10–15
Arm Curls	2	10–15
Triceps Pushdowns	2	10–15
Leg Raises	3	25–50
Sit-Ups	3	25–50

SQUATS

Stand erect with a barbell across your shoulders (you should step underneath a barbell that is already supported on squatting standards to get the bar onto your shoulders). If the bar is not comfortable, place a towel or pad between the bar and your shoulders. Your foot spacing should be a little wider than shoulder width, with your heels elevated and your feet turned out slightly. Descend slowly, with your back flat and chest held high, until the tops of your thighs are parallel to the floor or slightly lower. Then push right back up. Do not pause in the low position; always keep your legs tensed and body under control. Never round your back or attempt to use heavy weights until you master this technique. Wear a belt when you squat and always use spotters. Exhale as you come up and inhale as you descend.

A FIRST-DAY SAMPLE PROGRAM

Exercise	Sets	Reps
Giant Set One:		
Squats	1	12–20
Lunges	1	12–20
Leg Extensions	1	12–20
Leg Curls	1	12–20

Repeat Giant Set One three more times. Then do these basic bodybuilding exercises.

Exercise	Sets	Reps
Bench Presses	2	10–15
Lat Machine Pulls	2	10–15
Shoulder Presses	2	10–15
Arm Curls	2	10–15
Triceps Pushdowns	2	10–15
Leg Raises	3	25–50
Sit-Ups	3	25–50

LUNGES

Stand erect with a light barbell across your shoulders, or, alternatively, holding on to a pair of dumbbells. Take a step forward and sink slowly into a squat position, keeping the back leg straight. Then, contract your leg muscles to push yourself back upright. Do all your repetitions for one leg before reversing positions and doing your reps with your other leg. I also suggest that when you push yourself back up that you do not *quite* push yourself all the way up. This will force your muscles to work constantly and you'll get better development. Inhale as you lower yourself and exhale as you push yourself up.

LEG EXTENSIONS

Sit upright on an appropriate apparatus with your ankles and lower leg behind the apparatus pads as shown in the leg extension picture. Anchor yourself with your hands and slowly extend your lower legs, bringing the weight up until your legs are in a fully extended position. Lower the weight slowly and under control and then repeat the procedure. Do not arch your lower back and attempt to swing the weight up. Exhale as you raise the weight, inhale as you slowly lower the weight.

A FIRST-DAY SAMPLE PROGRAM

Exercise	Sets	Reps
Giant Set One:		
Squats	1	12–20
Lunges	1	12–20
Leg Extensions	1	12–20
Leg Curls	1	12–20

Repeat Giant Set One three more times. Then do these basic bodybuilding exercises.

Bench Presses	2	10–15
Lat Machine Pulls	2	10–15
Shoulder Presses	2	10–15
Arm Curls	2	10–15
Triceps Pushdowns	2	10–15
Leg Raises	3	25–50
Sit-Ups	3	25–50

A FIRST-DAY SAMPLE PROGRAM

Exercise	Sets	Reps
Giant Set One:		
Squats	1	12–20
Lunges	1	12–20
Leg Extensions	1	12–20
Leg Curls	1	12–20

Repeat Giant Set One three more times. Then do these basic bodybuilding exercises.

Bench Presses	2	10–15
Lat Machine Pulls	2	10–15
Shoulder Presses	2	10–15
Arm Curls	2	10–15
Triceps Pushdowns	2	10–15
Leg Raises	3	25–50
Sit-Ups	3	25–50

STANDING LEG CURLS

Stand erect with your lower ankles in front of a special pad. Supporting your upper body, curl one lower leg up until your heel approaches your butt. You may have to lean slightly forward to facilitate full movement. Alternate legs. Do not jerk the weight up. Instead, slowly curl each leg up with the power of your hamstrings alone. Do not cheat and arch your back or lean way forward to use your low back muscles. Lower the weight very slowly, under full control. Inhale as you lift the weight, exhale as you lower it.

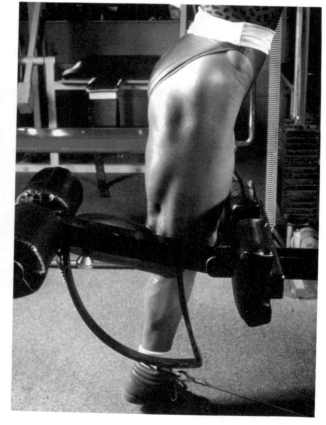

Be sure to use the right amount of weight. This means your weights should get too heavy to handle with good form somewhere between your twelfth and twentieth rep. If you can do only five reps, the weight's too heavy. If you can do 30, it's too light. Experiment a little to determine the appropriate poundages for you.

In addition to your specific thigh program, I suggest you also do a few other basic bodybuilding exercises. Do two or three sets of 10–15 repetitions of the following exercises: Leg Raises, Sits-Ups, Lat Machine Pulldowns, Bench Presses, Arm Curls, Shoulder Presses and Triceps Pushdowns.

You could do this workout on Monday, then on Wednesday do this same program substituting Giant Set Two. On Friday, the same plan using Giant Set Three. On Saturday, the same with Giant Set Four. Always do your giant sets at the start of your workout. Remember, do this bodybuilding program four times a week *in addition* to your daily aerobics.

Following my total thigh-slimming plan, you will burn somewhere around 700 extra calories a day. This will put you on your way to firmness fast.

THE FIGHT-FAT-THIGHS DIET

If you have learned one dietary concept so far, it's that eating fat is deadly. You already know that fat yields more than two times the calories of equal amounts of protein and carbohydrates. You know that fats are hidden in just about every food and you also know that fat is tempting because it provides feelings of fullness and satiety. So, if you are serious about toning and shaping thighs, avoid dietary fats like the plague!

Good eating means reorienting your nutritional thinking. Go ahead and eat a lot of natural, unrefined carbohydrates. You can (and should) eat breads, pasta, fruit, and potatoes. You can eat all the salads and vegetables you want, too. Make the most of your calories; make them carbohydrates and protein. Eat only when you are hungry. Snacking is no longer taboo. Just make sure that you snack on the correct foods.

One more thing; I encourage you to literally overdrink water throughout the day. This means you should drink at least 10–12 large glasses of water a day. This helps control your appetite and provides the necessary fluid medium for good health and proper digestion and absorption of nutrients. Water is a much-overlooked nutrient.

You should know all about nutrition now after reading chapter four. Pay attention to the list of slim and fat foods at the end of my book.

Even if your thighs have always been heavy, I refuse to believe that nothing can be done. Follow my exercise and diet guidelines and I *guarantee* you'll succeed! Competitive bodybuilders should refer to my leg training chapter later in this book.

6
TIGHT TUMMIES

When you look straight down at your toes, can you see them? If your toes aren't there, you might be in big trouble. When you think about it, is it any wonder our tummies get out of shape? After all, your abdomen is continually beseiged by butter, peanut butter, beer, and seas of salty french fries. And that's not good!

USE IT OR LOSE IT

You abdominals shouldn't be flabby. Often while your insides churn away digesting your food, your external abdominal muscles might be getting terribly weak. What should you do about it?

When you put a stick of butter, solid fat, into the sun, it melts, doesn't it. When you exercise you create heat and heat melts fat. We exercise our legs every day by walking and standing. Our arms and shoulders have to lift things all day. But what about the tummy? Most of the time, your abdominal muscles just go along for the ride. If you don't exercise your abdominal muscles directly, or indirectly in stabilizing movements that are a part of most athletic activities, you will get a protruding tummy.

As with our thighs, getting rid of tummy fat is no easy proposition. On our stomachs, it also sticks like glue. Not only is an overweight tummy an eyesore when we hit the beach, it sometimes causes medical problems.

Distension Blues

Your main abdominal muscle is your rectus abdominis, which runs from your lower ribcage down to your pelvis bones. When well developed, a bodybuilder's rectus abdominis is responsible for that rippled "washboard" look.

Underneath your rectus abdominis, and well-contained within its rigid walls, are your internal organs. There, some 30 feet of intestines and stomach digest, absorb, and help assimilate food. Should your rectus abdominis weaken and lose its muscle tone, it's easier for fat to accumulate.

Slowly, your intestines lose some of their motility power. Your stomach gets fat. Often you get indigestion and bloating simply because your tummy is trapped! Good muscle tone and proper eating prevent this every time.

Why do you suppose so many middle-aged adults develop bad backs? Yup, weak stomach muscles! Ask any doctor. This is the first thing she'll tell you! Envision, if you will, an old mare put out to pasture. Do you see the swayback from arthritic bone degradation? Now you get an idea what can happen to a middle-aged adult who does not exercise and eats like a horse.

An out-of-shape tummy (or one that has lost all semblance of muscle tone) allows your pelvis to assume a forward-tilted position. This is called lordosis, another name for swayback. With a pelvis that literally wants to fall out of place (or tilt), you eventually wedge your vertebrae together. When your vertebrae pinch together from a pelvic forward tilt, you put excessive pressure on your spinal disc fluid. If the fluid is pushed out of its normal position, it puts pressure on spinal nerves and ZAP! You gotta lotta pain!

Abdominal exercise and good eating prevent this.

WAIST-AWAY TO A SLIM TUMMY

To whittle away extra abdominal fat and tone up abdominal muscles, you need functional exercises and a slimmerizing smorgasbord. When all is done, though, specific exercises are the key to a sleek, tight tummy. So that you appreciate the parts of the engine you are about to tune, here is a brief anatomical primer.

Muscles of the Abdomen

Transversus Abdominis. This broad muscle is the deepest abdominal muscle and is often referred to as the stomach girdle. It covers your whole midsection, from side to side and top to bottom. It's the only abdominal muscle that does not directly flex or rotate your spine. Instead, it provides postural support for your abdominal organs and assists breathing.

Internal Obliques. These are deep muscles reponsible for rotating and flexing your spine. They run diagonally from your hipbones to your ribs and breastbone.

External Obliques. Provided your external obliques are well developed, they form a classical V-shape. The muscle fibers travel up and outward from your lower abdominal hipbone attachments to your lower eight ribs. They are activated any time you flex or rotate your spine.

Rectus Abdominis. These superficial abdominal muscles run vertically from your rib cage down to your pelvic bones. Your rectus is divided into upper and lower sections. The upper portion brings your upper body toward your legs in a sit-up exercise. The lower portion helps bring your legs up when you do a leg raise exercise. The rectus also flattens your back against the floor if you are lying on your back. Thus, it helps maintain a posterior pelvic tilt position.

To a certain extent, working your abdominals is just like working any other muscle group. If you want thicker, stronger abdominal muscles, you need to add resistance to all your abdominal exercises. Indeed, to get "bigger" abdominals, you must progressively overload them. If you have competitive aspirations, you'll need developed abdominals. It's not enough just to have a small waist, although this does help.

My goal has always been to develop a sleek, tight tummy rather than a thick, powerful one. Not only does this look better on the posing dais, but most observers will agree that it's a lot sexier! Therefore, I like to do higher repetitions with light weights, or no extra weight besides my body weight. I also train my abdominals in a fast, nonstop fashion. This training method molds endurance into my tummy and burns more calories. All of this adds to the slimming effect.

In my opinion, your abdominal muscles

need to be worked more often than other muscle groups. In this respect, they do differ somewhat from the other muscles you train. I have no doubt that different muscle groups respond differently to varying frequencies. It's difficult to overtrain abdominals, calves, and forearms. On the other hand, it's easy to overtrain the chest, deltoids, legs, and arms.

Furthermore, examining most athletes' abdominals in comparison to their other body parts, one immediately realizes that their abdominals are usually more developed. This supports my theory that your abdominals can be trained frequently. Competitive sprinters, jumpers, wrestlers, and swimmers invariably have outstanding abdominal muscles. Likewise, I think my early sports participation contributed to my present waist development.

Tummy Training

Even if I'm not in my competitive season, I still work my abdominals three times a week. However, my training is not as long or as intense as it is in the three months before competition. Then I train my waist nearly every day.

To eliminate fat and tone your abdominals, you really only need to do three things: Follow a low-fat, even-calorie diet, and do two abdominal exercises, Abdominal Crunches and Leg Raises, five times a week. Do these while keeping your lower back flat against the floor. If you do three sets of 10–50 repetitions or more of these two exercises and make a conscious effort to eat correctly, you'll shape up your abdominals in three months or less, even if you are quite overweight when you start! During my noncompetitive season, I stick with Abdominal Crunches and Leg Raises at the end of my workouts, usually 2–4 times a week. This keeps my abdominals trim all year long. Three months before my contest, though— that's when I really lower the boom on them. That's when all extra fat has to go.

WINNING ABDOMINALS: MY WAY

Bodybuilding is a sport of balance. You will not do well if you have severe structural flaws or if some of your body parts are well developed while others are weak. Too many bodybuilders fail to understand that you should develop your musculature to highlight your structural strengths and downplay genetic weaknesses.

As an example, let's say you have wide hips and a short torso. Then you should avoid developing thick abdominals and you should also downplay your obliques. Thick abs and obliques give the illusion of heaviness and width, just the opposite of what you want. Instead, you should stress your upper rectus, intercostals, and serratus muscles. As I mentioned before, avoid using extra resistance with your abdominal exercises if your waistline is wide and boxy-looking.

I have a small waist genetically. Still, I concentrate on all my abdominal muscles as well as my serratus muscles on the upper, outer section of my abdominal wall. Although the serratus muscles are not technically part of your abdominal structure, they appear to be when they are fully developed. You can develop these muscles with pressing and pullover movements.

I like high repetitions with abdominals and I like to work them fast and continuously, like a machine plugging away. I do them the same way I recommend for thigh slimming—as one big, nonstop giant set. I use five exercises and I suggest that you do them the same way and in the same order as listed.

GIANT SET ABDOMINAL EXERCISES

PULLDOWN CRUNCHES

This movement is really a kind of a reverse crunch and is super effective. Do these on a lat machine pulldown station, positioning yourself on your knees. I prefer to hold the handle behind my head, pulling it slowly down until my chest hits the top of my thighs. I hold the bottom position for two seconds, tightening my abdominals in an isometric contraction. Then I slowly go back to the starting position, slightly resisting as I do with the tension in my abdominals. Exhale as you pull the weight down and inhale as you return to the starting position.

I do 25–40 repetitions. Most of the time I pull straight down, but occasionally I like to pull off to the side in an alternating fashion. This exercise works your rectus abdominis, serratus, and obliques. It's a good one that is frequently ignored in tummy trimming programs.

DECLINE SIT-UPS

Start easy on this one! Sometimes this can bother your back, so experiment first. Generally, I do sets of 50 repetitions with a 25-pound plate in my lap. Then I drop the plate off and continue for another 50 reps. I didn't start like this, though, and neither should you. Just start off with a few repetitions and gradually increase.

Assume a sitting position on an adjustable sit-up board set on a decline with your feet anchored. Try to keep your knees slightly bent. Tighten your stomach muscles and slowly lower yourself back until you are flat. Without relaxing, come back up to the starting position with the power of your abdominal muscles. Inhale as you go back and exhale as you actually complete the sit-up. Do not bounce, and exercise at a slow, steady pace.

I concentrate on curling up very slowly, trying to isolate my abdominals. Your hip flexor muscles are also involved, so you must concentrate very hard on using only your abdominals. This exercise works your lower abdominals as well as your upper abs.

LEG RAISES OFF THE BENCH

Sit on the end of a bench with your upper body inclined slightly backward. Tighten your abdominals and slowly raise your legs off the floor until your feet are as high as your head. Make sure that you keep your legs straight or you will put the stress on your upper hips rather than your lower abdominals. Do not just let your legs flop back down, but lower them to the starting position with a constant contraction of your abdominals. Inhale as you lower your legs and exhale when you lift them up.

I like, and I suggest, 10–40 repetitions through a full range of motion.

45-DEGREE TWISTS

This is another good exercise that is ignored. That's too bad because it's my main internal and external oblique exercise. On a sit-up board or a flat bench, simply anchor your feet, lean back, and twist away. Now, I do this with a weighted bar across my shoulders (usually no more than 15 pounds), but it's very effective with just your body weight as resistance. However, it won't be effective if you don't lean backward.

Twist fully to one side and then the other. Twist slowly, keeping a constant tension on your abdominals. I do 50–100 repetitions, but again, I worked up to this slowly. You need to do only what you are capable of at first and gradually increase! Another little tip: at the end of each twist, exhale forcibly and try to "cramp" your side with a super-hard flexion of the muscles. This will add a touch of definition to the area.

CRUNCHES

The old standby! I always finish my routine
with crunches. I suggest you do the same.
This exercise works your upper rectus abdominis. I do 40-80 repetitions, but the main thing
is to work for a good, burning sensation in
your abdominals.

Lie on a flat bench or the floor with your
knees bent and feet raised up. You can lie
crossways to a bench and place your bent
legs up on the bench or hold them up with
your thigh muscles. From a flat torso position,
slowly curl your upper body toward your knees
as if to crunch your body together. Make sure
you come up high enough so that your
shoulder blades clear the floor, but not much
beyond that. Do all your crunches slowly and
as you do them, concentrate on pushing your
lower back into the floor or bench. Exhale as
you do the crunch; inhale as you slowly lower
yourself back to the flat starting position.

I do one set of all five of these exercises
in a row in back-to-back fashion. I then come
back and repeat the five-exercise giant set
two or three more times. This is one good abdominal workout and it'll shape you up fast.

My abdominal philosophy is based on an overriding concept: When you train, work with nature. If God gave you narrow shoulders and a wide waistline structurally, create an illusion of narrowness. Forget heavy dumbbell side bends and weighted sit-ups. Forget chunky abdominals. Overdevelop your latissimus and deltoids. Do high repetitions and multiple sets. Train in a giant set, nonstop fashion. Concentrate. And, if you want that small waist, that trim tummy, pretend you're that stick of butter in the sun. Create some heat. Move through your abdominal exercises like you really mean it. Eventually, you'll get a waistline you can really be proud to call your own!

7
SHAPELY BREASTS

It's generally agreed by athletes everywhere that fat is undesirable. Of course, if you are a sumo wrestler, we make exceptions. There is one place, however, where fat is acceptable: the female breast!

Despite advertisements to the contrary, there is no direct way to increase the size or shape of your breasts other than by gaining body weight. Your breasts are composed of fat and glands and not much else. Changing the actual breast cup size, then, is almost totally dependent upon changes in your weight.

Many women suffer psychologically from small breasts. Most of this can be blamed on commercial interests. Think about it. People have actually become wealthy over breasts. Jayne Mansfield made a fortune on hers and Hugh Hefner hasn't done so badly exploiting breasts either. Certain plastic surgeons would also qualify.

Women have tried all kinds of useless creams, fancy lotions, topical hormones, and special devices in a fruitless effort to enlarge their breasts. However, short of plastic surgery, the only way to improve or change your breast appearance is indirectly, through diet and exercise.

YOU CAN'T TELL A BOOK BY ITS COVER

Our image of the perfect pair of breasts is patently false. Most models who appear nude or who otherwise model their bosoms have undergone some kind of breast implantation surgery. Or their photos have undergone extensive airbrush retouching. As of 1981, the American Society of Plastic Surgeons revealed that breast implantation was the most frequently performed plastic surgery. It is estimated by some that in 1987, nearly 250,000 implant operations will be done!

SURGEON-SCULPTED VOLUPTUOUSNESS

Breast implant surgery is not new and many models as well as bodybuilders are interested in this subject. Surgeons have attempted to enlarge female breasts since before World War II. In those days, surgeons used abdominal and buttock fat to form chest grafts. Later, silicone injections became increasingly popular until the United States Food and Drug Administration banned silicone injections because they were potentially dangerous. Today, surgeons use different types of implants of varying sizes to augment breast shape.

Implantation isn't cheap. Typically, implant surgery varies from $2,000 to $4,000 as surgeon's fees, anesthesia, and facility costs differ widely. Surgeons place an implant into your body through different routes, too. Some surgeons prefer to place the implant in through the patient's nipple-areolar complex. However, this area must be large enough for the surgeon to make this approach. Because of all the sensitive nerves in this area there may be residual loss of sensitivity following the surgery.

Another method of approach is underneath the body of the breast. With this approach, the resultant scar is partially hidden in the natural breast fold, whereas, with the nipple-areolar approach, the scar is hidden by the difference in color in comparison to the rest of the breast.

A final approach is underneath the patient's arm in the axilla area. This is a more difficult procedure, but offers the best hiding place for the scar. Many models who pose nude have opted for this method of implant induction.

Implants are placed either on top of or underneath the pectoralis major muscle. Placing an implant over the muscle is probably an easier surgery and this method has been more common in the past and probably still is today. However, more and more surgeons seem to favor the under-the-muscle approach as the pectoralis muscle can then act as a dynamic force helping prevent the formation of scar tissue after surgery.

An implant is a foreign body and as such your body reacts to it by forming protective scar tissue. If too much scar tissue forms, the implant loses its pliability, becoming contracted with hard scar tissue. Some surgeons insist this is less likely when the implant is placed under the muscle. Others debate this contention. At any rate, exercise,

external massage, and flexibility work to help prevent or minimize scar tissue formation.

When you bodybuild competitively, you become very lean. If you have a breast implant on top of the muscle, this will be visible once you get into top shape. Female bodybuilders should consider this if they want such surgery. On the other side of the coin, placing an implant underneath the muscle means that some muscle fibers must be cut. The surgeon also has to contend with the dynamic nature of the pectoralis contraction during posing. This may make the implant harder to fit. At present, I would estimate that 20% of top professional bodybuilders have implants. The rate for professional models might be around 70%!

As with any surgery, complications can arise. With breast surgery, one complication could be loss of the ability to breastfeed. Be sure to consider this when you make your decision.

Smaller Breasts

The Legendary Amazon warriors were reputed to have had one of their breasts removed to become better archers. Horror stories notwithstanding, you might be surprised that many women want smaller breasts for health and comfort.

It is possible to reduce breast size by losing body fat, especially if you are significantly overweight. However, this process is limited and for women with really large breasts, breast reduction surgery might be an answer to a prayer.

Female athletes with large breasts may experience discomfort during competition and training. Breast reduction (unlike implant surgery) is usually covered by standard medical insurance because this operation is most often performed for health rather than cosmetic purposes.

Unlike implantation, breast reduction does not increase your chances for developing breast cancer or tumors. However, with either of these surgeries, especially reduction, your ability to lactate and breast-feed children may be lost.

Of course, not everyone would resort to surgery to change bust size. Surgery of this sort is not to be taken lightly. Besides, most women can increase their breast size *indirectly* by enlarging muscles that lift the chest wall, giving the whole bosom a fuller, larger appearance.

ADDING A LIFT TO YOUR BOSOM

By increasing the muscle tone in your pectoralis major and minor and serratus anterior muscles, you can lift up your rib cage and breasts. This is especially so if you concentrate on your upper pectoralis. If you are round-shouldered, you can improve your posture and indirectly your breast appearance by improving the muscle tone of your upper back muscles (rhomboids, teres group, and trapezius group).

On a basic level, Push-Ups and shoulder shrugging exercises (hold books in your hands for added resistance) will improve posture and breast carriage. To start building muscle tone in your chest, you can simply do three sets of as many push-ups as you can four times a week. On opposite days do the shrugging exercise, three sets of 25–50 repetitions each.

Formal bodybuilding programs are even better. Here's a program that I recommend to begin to increase your breast size. Do this three or four times a week:

Exercise	Sets	Reps
Incline Dumbbell Presses	2	15–20
Incline Dumbbell Flyes	2	15–20
Cable Crossover or Pec-dec Machine Flyes	2	15–20
Long Pulley Rows	2	15–20
Upright Rows	2	15–20

Always warm up first. Use the maximum training weight that you can in good form for the required repetitions. If you follow this program and do some abdominal and lung-expanding aerobic work, you will get results.

I'm sure most of you are more concerned with your whole chest, not just breast size. If you are interested in increasing the size, strength, and definition of your chest muscles, I've got just the thing for you, too!

BUILDING A TREASURE CHEST

Most bodybuilders discover that their chest muscles respond readily to exercise. Your pectorals are thick, flat, broad, and powerful. The "pecs" bring your arms together in front of your body, and when you're lying on your back, they are responsible for pushing objects away from your chest.

Pectorals seem to respond because they aren't used much in normal daily activities. Instead, we use our deltoid, biceps, and triceps muscles much more frequently. Because training stress is new and different to your pectorals, they respond quickly.

Still, gaining muscle size is always the main problem for a majority of women bodybuilders. Since pressing motions utilize the biggest muscle masses, those are the ones you should concentrate on. The pressing exercises that work the upper pectorals are the most important of all.

Neophyte Chest Training

A beginner should always work her chest as part of a whole-body workout. Three times a week is best, allowing you to develop proper motor pathways (skill) and slowly condition your chest for higher workloads to follow. Remember, always work your biggest muscle groups toward the beginning of your workout when your energy is highest. Always use the heaviest weight possible for the required repetitions. Here is a novice chest plan broken down by training days.

MONDAY

Exercise	Sets	Reps
Low-Incline Dumbbell Presses	3	10–15
Flat-Bench Dumbbell Presses	2–3	10–15
Incline Dumbbell Flyes	2	15–20

WEDNESDAY

Exercise	Sets	Reps
Incline Barbell Presses	3	10–12
Flat-Bench Barbell Presses	2	10–12

FRIDAY

Exercise	Sets	Reps
Incline Dumbbell Presses	3	8–12

Variety in your exercise routine allows you to make continuous progress. By decreasing your workload toward the end of the week, you decrease the chances of overtraining. Work your chest first. Follow chest exercises with exercises for shoulders, back, and arms in that order. Take a rest and then work your legs and abdominals.

As I mentioned in my "Nuts and Bolts" chapter, you must learn to *feel* the way your muscles respond to an exercise to develop maximum size and shape. This is critical. Those who don't learn to exercise by feel never make it big as bodybuilders. It's no different with your pectorals.

On all your pressing motions, inhale as you lower the weight and exhale as you push it up. When you do flyes, inhale as you lower and exhale as your arms come together.

If pressing with a bar, lower it to the high point of your expanded chest. Push it up with your elbows pointing outward, not held in. Keep your upper arms perpendicular to your body to emphasize your chest muscles. Feel the stretch. The same is true when pressing dumbbells. Lower them to the sides of your chest, as far down as you can, to get a good stretch. Keep your palms pronated (facing straight ahead).

When doing flyes, concentrate on keeping constant tension on your pectorals. Never relax, always flex. With flyes, style takes precedence over weight—always.

Work hard on the incline presses. Women wear bikini tops. We don't need great lower pecs. We need great upper pecs!

Exercise	Sets	Reps
Low-Incline Dumbbell Presses	3	10–15
Flat-Bench Dumbbell Presses	2–3	10–15
Incline Dumbbell Flyes	2	15–20

LOW-INCLINE DUMBBELL PRESSES

Position yourself on a 35-degree incline bench with two dumbbells on the floor, one on each side of the incline bench. Bend down and lift the dumbbells up so that you're lying down on the incline bench with the dumbbells in position to press up. Exhale and push the dumbbells up at the same time. Keep your elbows directed out to your sides so the emphasis is on your chest muscles. Inhale and lower the dumbbells together and press them up again for a complete repetition, exhaling as you push them up.

Exercise	Sets	Reps
Low-Incline Dumbbell Presses	3	10–15
Flat-Bench Dumbbell Presses	2–3	10–15
Incline Dumbbell Flyes	2	15–20

FLAT-BENCH DUMBBELL PRESSES

Lie on your back so you feel stable holding the dumbbells off to the sides of your body, then push them up. Always keep your elbows directed out to the sides for maximum stress to your chest. Never hold your breath when doing presses—exhale as you push the weights up and inhale as you let them down.

Exercise	Sets	Reps
Low-Incline Dumbbell Presses	3	10–15
Flat-Bench Dumbbell Presses	2–3	10–15
Incline Dumbbell Flyes	2	15–20

INCLINE DUMBBELL FLYES

On an incline bench, assume the same position you would if you were going to press the dumbbells overhead. For flyes, however, hold the dumbbells with your palms facing each other. Inhale as you lower them slowly, keeping your elbows bent slightly. While exhaling bring the dumbbells back up through the same arc along which you lowered them. Never swing the dumbbells up.

INTERMEDIATE CHEST TRAINING

After six months of pec-blasting, it's time to upgrade your program to ensure continued progress. Go to a four-day-a-week split system, training your upper body twice a week and lower body twice a week. This will allow you to add more sets and exercises of chest work. You will now have the time to do so.

As a suggested example, you could train on Monday, Tuesday, Thursday, and Friday. On Monday and Thursday, do all your upper body exercises, on Tuesday and Friday, all your lower body exercises. Here's a specific recommendation for the chest section of your upper body:

Compare this program to the beginner's routine. When you move up to the intermediate level, you upgrade both the volume and intensity of your training. Just as Frank Shorter trains harder than someone just starting the marathon, intermediate bodybuilders train harder and longer than novices. Don't let anyone tell you different!

Doing more exercises and sets ensures that your pectorals won't accommodate themselves to fixed physiological demands, exercise loads or angles and stop growing. Remember, a holistic approach means better development all the way around.

INTERMEDIATE CHEST WORKOUT
TUESDAY

Exercise	Sets	Reps
High-Incline Dumbbell Presses	3–4	10–12
Low-Incline Dumbbell Presses	3–4	10–12
Flat-Bench Presses	3	8–12

Follow with your shoulder, back, and arm exercises.

THURSDAY

Exercise	Sets	Reps
Incline-Bar Presses	4	8–12
Low-Incline Dumbbell Presses	3	10–12
Flat-Bench Presses	2–3	15–20

Continue with shoulder, back, and arm exercises.

INTERMEDIATE CHEST WORKOUT
TUESDAY

Exercise	Sets	Reps
High-Incline Dumbbell Presses	3–4	10–12
Low-Incline Dumbbell Presses	3–4	10–12
Flat-Bench Presses	3	8–12

HIGH-INCLINE DUMBBELL PRESSES

Position yourself on a 75-degree incline bench with two dumbbells on the floor, one on each side of the incline bench. Bend down and lift the dumbbells up so that you are lying down on the incline bench with the dumbbells in position to press up. Exhale and push the dumbbells up at the same time. Keep your elbows directed out to your sides so the emphasis is on your chest muscles. Inhale and lower the dumbbells together and press them up again. This is like the Low-Incline Dumbbell Press, but emphasizes a different part of the chest muscles.

INTERMEDIATE CHEST WORKOUT
TUESDAY

Exercise	Sets	Reps
High-Incline Dumbbell Presses	3–4	10–12
Low-Incline Dumbbell Presses	3–4	10–12
Flat-Bench Presses	3	8–12

FLAT-BENCH BARBELL PRESSES

Lie on your back on a flat exercise bench with support standards. Position yourself under the bar and keep your body stable. Take a slightly wider than shoulder-width grip on the barbell, palms facing up. Lift the barbell up and, under control, slowly lower it to the high point of your chest. Without pausing push the bar back up. Never hold your breath when doing presses. Exhale as you push the bar up and inhale as you lower the bar. Always keep your elbows directed out to the sides for maximum stress to your chest muscles.

Advanced Chest Training

Progress is always slow, but steady. After a year of pushing and pulling iron you are ready to work on an advanced chest program. This will be much more strenuous. Only after allowing yourself a year of chest training will you be able to tell if you can take this. It takes more time, motivation and energy. Once again, you significantly increase both the volume and intensity of your training.

I know what you're thinking. Some of you have read that advanced bodybuilders don't need more training—they just need more intense training. I disagree, as would most bodybuilders. Advanced athletes always need to train longer and harder to improve. Why does a younger golfer overtake an older one? Because the younger golfer is hungrier and practices more. Sure, there is a certain level of skill degradation with age in many sports, but that's not a factor in bodybuilding.

How do you think 55-year-old champion Albert Beckles manages to keep ahead of the pack? By training harder and longer (up to six hours a day!) than everyone else. Yes, some advanced bodybuilders actually make better gains training three times a week, but these fortunate individuals are few and far between.

Standard fare for most advanced bodybuilders is once-a-day training for most of the off-season (the noncompetitive portion of the training year). Then, some 2–4 months before a contest, they start training twice a day utilizing the double-split system pioneered by Joe Weider.

I train twice a day year round, except for three months of active vacation immediately following the Ms. Olympia. I use the popular three-days-on/one-day-off system. Not only can I handle such a severe system, I seem to thrive on it. Ultimately, only you can be the final judge of the severity of your workload. This takes experimenting. The fact that everyone seems to respond differently to different programs is the basis of the Instinctive Training Principle (also pioneered by Joe Weider).

The main advantage to a double-split system is training time. With more time per week spent training, you can handle a higher volume of sets and repetitions. More sets mean better pecs. By adding different exercises, you are able to work your chest from varying angles for better shape, too. Here's a more advanced split system organized according to body parts. You'll train each part two times a week using a three-days-on one-day-off system.

Monday: Pectorals, deltoids, and triceps
Tuesday: Thighs, low back, calves, and abdominals
Wednesday: Upper back, biceps, and abdominals
Thursday: Rest day
Friday: Start the three day cycle over again

MONDAY AND FRIDAY

Exercise	Sets	Reps
High-Incline Dumbbell Presses	4	8–15
Low-Incline Dumbbell Presses	4	10–15
Flat-Bench Presses	4–5	8–12
High-Incline Dumbbell Flyes	4–5	15–20

Another way to use the split system is with a two-days-on/one-day-off schedule, training once each workout day, working more body parts during each session, as follows:

Monday: Pectorals, deltoids, upper back, and abdominals.
Tuesday: Thighs, low back, biceps, triceps, and calves
Wednesday: Rest day
Thursday: Start the two-day cycle over again

Under this system, you work your chest every third day, starting with Monday, Thursday, and Sunday and just continuing according to the rotation cycle.

MONDAY AND FRIDAY MORNING ROUTINE

Exercise	Sets	Reps	Weight (lbs.)
Low-Incline Dumbbell Presses	1	20	45
	1	15	60
	1	12	70
	1	10	75
	1	15	60
High-Incline Dumbbell Presses	1	20	45
	4	15	55
Flat-Bench Presses	1	20	95
	1	15	145
	1	12	165
	1	8–10	185
	1	15	145
Cable Crossovers or Dumbbell Flyes	4	15–20	

DUMBBELL FLYES

You may do flyes either on a flat or incline bench. If you do flyes on a bench, assume the same position you would if you were going to press the dumbbells overhead. This time, though, hold the dumbbells with your palms facing each other. Take a big inhalation, then lower both dumbbells to the sides while keeping your elbows slightly bent. Go down slowly and under control, making sure to feel a good stretch to your chest muscles. Exhale and bring the dumbbells back up to the starting position along the exact same arc through which you lowered them.

CABLE CROSSOVERS (FLYES)

With Standing Cable Crossovers (Flyes), you grasp the handles with each hand and pull the resistance down and across your body while leaning ever so slightly forward. Keeping your body in the same position, slowly resist the handles going back to the starting position and then pull them down again. Exhale as you pull the handles down and inhale as you return to the starting position.

Here is the way I currently work my chest using a double-split, three-days-on/one-day-off approach (working out twice a day):

Monday
A.M.: Chest and abdominals
P.M.: Back

Tuesday
A.M.: Quadriceps and abdominals
P.M.: Hamstrings,calves, and low back

Wednesday
A.M.: Shoulders and abdominals
P.M.: Arms

Thursday
Rest Day

Friday
A.M.: Chest and abdominals
P.M.: Back

I don't worry about the weight with my flyes. Instead, I concentrate on strict technique. On most of the others, though, I'm conscious of what weight I use and the number of reps that I want to achieve. This is crucial for continued growth.

I never do fewer than 20 sets and sometimes go as high as 30 sets. On most of my chest exercises I follow an ascending and descending pyramid approach. As I increase the weight I do fewer repetitions. Then, when I lower the weight I do more repetitions. I use a high-rep warm-up set on my pressing movements to "get the feel" of each exercise. I always use the heaviest weight I can for the repetitions I want. This ensures that I train with maximum intensity.

Flat-bench exercises tie in my chest-delt area and hit my central and lower pectorals. The incline work at different areas builds my upper chest. Cable Crossovers or Dumbbell Flyes stress my pectorals as they tie in to my sternum.

If you follow my plans, your chest muscles will respond quickly. Remember, your delts, pecs, and triceps are all affected by many of the same exercises. Therefore, avoid trying too much too soon. Never overtrain. Start slowly at your own level and progress gradually. Eventually, you'll achieve the chest development you seek—whether it be a shapelier chest, a larger bosom, smaller bosom, or the competitive chest development of a bodybuilding champion.

8
POWERFUL ARMS

Have you ever carried a bag of groceries less than a city block, but barely made it to your destination because your arms and shoulders felt like they were going to explode from fatigue? It shouldn't be this way. More than any other muscles, your arms and shoulders should be synonymous with strength, even if you're a woman! This doesn't mean that you need biceps that embarrass Mr. Universe. Besides, even if you desired huge arm muscles, it would be an impossible task.

Having strength means you have enough muscle tone to carry a bag of groceries. It means having enough power to turn the lug nuts so you can change a flat tire. It means having the strength to open a jar of pickles. It means that your arms are not so skinny that they're mistaken for coat hangers.

You can develop muscle tone in your arms and shoulders—even if you've been a life-long weakling. Believe me, Push-Ups alone will do wonders. You don't have to use barbells and dumbbells if you don't want to. It's just that they are the most efficient way.

It's okay to do Push-Ups the way we were

taught in girls' P.E. (you know, on your knees). You can start doing women's Push-Ups four times a week. Just do four sets of as many repetitions as you can three or four times a week. Once you can knock off 25 of them with ease, you should get off your knees and on your toes and do Push-Ups the regular way. Still do three or four sets of as many repetitions as you can, three or four days a week. Push-Ups are a great toning exercise for your chest, shoulders, and the back of your arms.

What about your biceps? You can do the same exercise routine by curling a couple of books. Hopefully, it won't be the only use for your family Bible or encyclopedia! If you want more than the beginning inklings of shoulder and arm muscle tone, you can use dumbbells.

A pair of adjustable dumbbells can be miracle workers. By purchasing a set that can range from 10–30 pounds you can do anything.

To achieve a level of muscle tone comparable to the Push-Up and book curls routine I described above, do the following:

Exercise	Sets	Reps	Weight (lbs.)
Dumbbell Curls	1	20	10
	1	15	15
	1	10	15–20
Overhead Presses (one arm at a time)	1	15	10
	1	10	15
	1	10	20

If you are too weak to handle this much weight, you have a lot of work to do, but it's okay. Bodybuilding is individual—all relative to yourself. No matter where you are, you will quickly gain muscle tone and strength.

I suggest doing this simple routine three times a week and adding a few Push-Ups to it. The routine won't take longer than 20–30 minutes. At this level of intensity, you will tone up without adding muscle size.

Serious bodybuilders soon discover that, unlike some muscles, arm size is not easy to develop. Your biceps (for simplicity, I will refer to your elbow flexors as biceps even though there are also other muscles involved) and triceps (elbow extensors) are not extremely complicated muscles. Basically, your biceps lifts your forearm up to your shoulder and helps turn your palms up. Your triceps straightens your arms out from a bent position. Bodybuilders can do a variety of exercises to build up their arms without having to get fancy.

BICEPS MANIA

The media have always liked to *pretend* that all male bodybuilders flock to the beach and strut around preening their pumped, oiled biceps like peacocks. I don't know how this image developed. Even the male bodybuilders who gathered at Santa Monica's Muscle Beach *years ago* cared less about showing their biceps than they did practicing gymnastics and hand-balancing. Me? I hate going to the beach and the *only* time I

flex my biceps is in a contest. That's the way I like it.

Biceps mania is a vice anyway. In the first place, muscle proportion is still the most important criterion for winning. It'll do you no good to have big biceps with dinky triceps. You need to develop both.

Secondly, size doesn't mean much without shape and definition. Those members of the beefcake set who don't obtain correct shape and muscle definition *always* lose out. In the past Ms. Olympia contests, there were several women with bigger biceps than mine. It didn't matter.

Although it's good to work hard on your biceps and triceps, remember, their combined mass is small when compared to your chest, back, or legs. Too many aspiring bodybuilders delude themselves that big biceps and triceps is where it's at. Not so. The upper arm is only one body part and a small one at that. You simply cannot spend all your time on arms. It's not worth the labor. Whatever time you do spend on arms, you want to get the most return. Here's how—whether you're a novice, intermediate, or advanced bodybuilder.

Remember, my definition of a novice is someone who trains three times a week with free weights, with less than six months' experience. A beginner should do two exer-

cises for her biceps and one for her triceps. Why only one for the triceps? After all, I'm sure you have read elsewhere that the triceps comprises two-thirds of the mass of your upper arm and therefore should be trained harder and more frequently.

However, whenever you do a pressing exercise for your deltoids or chest, your triceps is directly activated. It's an easy muscle to overtrain (and thus stall progress). As a beginner, you should work your biceps and triceps at the end of your other upper body work.

Even if it seems your arms are responding slowly, don't attempt more because you'll overtrain them for sure. You'll be on the beginning routine for only six months and you must accommodate to workloads of progressive severity.

BEGINNING ARM TRAINING
Monday, Wednesday, and Friday

Exercise	Sets	Reps
Barbell Curls	3	10–15
Alternate Dumbbell Curls	2	10–15
Triceps Pushdowns	3	10–15

STANDING BARBELL CURLS

Stand erect while holding either a straight or EZ-curl bar with your arms extended in front of your body holding the bar against your thighs. Hold the bar with a supinated, palms-up grip. Keeping your elbows close to your sides, slowly curl the bar toward your neck. Do not swing the bar up. Inhale as you raise the bar, exhale as you lower it. Start with an approximate shoulder-width grip.

BEGINNING ARM TRAINING
Monday, Wednesday, and Friday

Exercise	Sets	Reps
Barbell Curls	3	10–15
Alternate Dumbbell Curls	2	10–15
Triceps Pushdowns	3	10–15

ALTERNATE DUMBBELL CURLS

You may stand or sit. Hold a dumbbell in each hand. Inhale and curl one dumbbell up to your shoulder. Exhale and lower the same dumbbell to the starting position. Then, inhale and raise the other dumbbell to your shoulder in a curling motion. Exhale and lower. Repeat with each arm for the required repetitions.

I suggest that you wear a lifting belt for both standing or seated curls. You also might find turning your palms out slightly as you curl will benefit your development.

BEGINNING ARM TRAINING
Monday, Wednesday, and Friday

Exercise	Sets	Reps
Barbell Curls	3	10–15
Alternate Dumbbell Curls	2	10–15
Triceps Pushdowns	3	10–15

TRICEPS PUSHDOWNS

Stand erect facing a lat machine weight stack. Grasp a bar hooked to the cable, using an overhead grip. Keeping your elbows in or out (you should do it both ways), press down on the bar slowly and steadily until your elbows are completely extended. Slowly let the weight back and repeat. Do not jerk the weight down. Breathe normally.

VARIETY IS THE SPICE OF LIFE ... AND GOOD ARMS!

Once you've developed an understanding of bodybuilding technique and you've built up a tolerance for a higher workload, you can change routines to realize your maximum potential. Only by stressing your muscles from every possible angle can you ensure that you will achieve maximum development. Your muscles work together in different movements and are affected differently with alternate motions.

When you reach an intermediate stage of training, you'll be able to work with a routine that allows more time on specific body parts. An intermediate bodybuilder should still work her arms last, after bigger muscle groups. The exception to this is someone, for whatever reason, who has very good development of her other body parts, but lags horribly in the arms department.

In this case, you could train your arms at the beginning of your program when your energy is highest. This is called muscle priority training.

Generally, though, you should do all your chest, shoulder, and back work first. This is where your greatest growth potential is. Here's my prescription for intermediate arm training on Mondays and Thursdays. (Remember, an intermediate is anyone with more than six months of regular training experience.)

This is about all the arm work an inter-mediate can handle, *especially* after working chest, shoulders, and back!

There's no reason you can't mix it up. On your second day, you might do your Scott curls first or maybe you could work triceps before biceps. This is where bodybuilding individuality comes into play. The most important points are:

1. Use the heaviest weight you can for the desired repetitions, but always emphasize strict technique.
2. Generally, work your biggest muscle groups at the start of your routine.

Anyone who bodybuilds for an appreciable time soon realizes how difficult it is to train four body parts in the same session. If you train chest, shoulders, back, and arms on the same day, you can be doing 40–45 sets! Obviously, this can lead to over-training.

Serious students of the game soon make the switch to a daily body part routine. Again, *most* bodybuilders train once on a workout day, usually following a three-days-on one-day-off schedule. Other bodybuilders like a double split, training twice a day, alternating body parts.

On the other hand, a few bodybuilders (champions, too), stay with a three-day-a-week or four-day-a-week program. All of these different schedules (even training twice a day, *every* day) might work. I can only offer my experience and guidance, but ultimately, you must determine the best system for yourself. If you can't do this, you won't realize your physical potential.

INTERMEDIATE ARM TRAINING
Monday and Thursday

Exercise	Sets	Reps
Barbell Curls	2–3	10–12
Scott Curls	2–3	10–12
Alternate Dumbbell Curls	2–3	10–15

Standing or lying on an incline bench.

Lying Triceps Extensions	3	10–15
Triceps Pushdowns	3	10–12

SCOTT CURLS

Position yourself over an inclined (preacher) bench so that your arms are nearly vertical. Using either a barbell or dumbbells and keeping your upper arms flat against the bench, curl the weight toward your shoulders. Always lower the weights slowly and breathe normally.

INTERMEDIATE ARM TRAINING
Monday and Thursday

Exercise	Sets	Reps
Barbell Curls	2–3	10–12
Scott Curls	2–3	10–12
Alternate Dumbbell Curls	2–3	10–15

Standing or lying on an incline bench.

Lying Triceps Extensions	3	10–15
Triceps Pushdowns	3	10–12

LYING TRICEPS EXTENSIONS

Lie on a bench holding an EZ-curl or regular barbell with a narrow, pronated grip. Press the bar straight up. Keeping your elbows stationary, lower the bar slowly to your forehead or further behind your head off the end of the bench. Once you have lowered the bar back as far as possible, extend your elbows so the bar is returned to the upright starting position. Breathe normally.

Typically, developing significant muscle size and good shape are the main goals of a serious female bodybuilder. It's not easy. I've repeatedly tried to point out that size is not everything and you should be concerned with shape and proportion as well.

For instance, let's say you've developed a good peak on your biceps, but the muscle isn't long and full. You would not want to do a lot of Concentration Curls (see next section for description), which are a peaking movement, but instead, spend a lot of time on Scott Curls, which stress your brachialis muscle. The brachialis lies under your lower biceps. Building a bigger brachialis will give the illusion of a longer biceps even though it's not even related.

Although your basic muscle shapes are fixed, you can create balance by building accessory muscles. Let me give you another arm example. Suppose your inner and outer triceps heads are well-developed, but your long head is not. The long head of your triceps crosses the axis of both your elbow and shoulder joints. As a two-jointed muscle, it does elbow joint and shoulder joint extension.

What does this mean to you? If you pre-flex your shoulder joint (as you would if you got in a seated or lying triceps extension position), you lengthen your triceps long head over the shoulder joint. When you lengthen a two-joint muscle over one of its joints, it can shorten or contract better over its other joint. This means your triceps long head now gets a better workout from elbow joint extension. You can isolate different heads of a multiple-joint muscle. This shapes your muscles.

You see why variety is important for optimum muscle shape. Advanced arm training means you train for size, proportion, and shape!

MY ADVANCED ARM TRAINING

I like to train my biceps and triceps together. Many bodybuilders will group their biceps with upper back since both sets of

muscle groups are "pullers." By training them together in the same session, you then ensure complete recovery before you hit pulling muscles again. You'll notice I suggest this in earlier sections of this book.

However, as I've also said before, you must find out what works best for *you* and you alone. I train my chest and abdominals in the morning and work my back in the evening. The next day I train my quadriceps and abdominals in the morning and my hamstrings, low back, and calves in the evening. My third training day involves shoulders and abs in the morning and my biceps and triceps in the evening. The fourth day I rest and on the fifth, I start anew.

Since my triceps are well-developed from my early years of heavy bench pressing and heaving eight-pound balls (shot-putting), I start my arm training with biceps. I have long arms. If you look like a gangling-goon (long arms and legs) you need to add extra muscle just to look as thick as a shorter bodybuilder. This is why I start with my biceps.

To reiterate, you need a variety of exercises, sets and repetitions (8–20) to develop every aspect of your muscle. I don't rest much between sets and I use the heaviest weights possible for my reps. One more thing, I don't cheat on my arm exercises. If you cheat and deviate from proper form, you'll end up working your front deltoids and upper back muscles more than your arms.

I only list my training weights so you get an example of progressions. Don't try to match my weights. What you lift is meaningful only to yourself. Comparisons mean nothing.

I do higher repetitions on my first and last sets. This approach works best for me. I use a pyramid system (raising and lowering the poundages) on the standing barbell curls.

I use forced repetitions (with my training partner's help) on the Scott Curls, but this is the only exercise for which I use them and I never do more than three assisted reps.

The barbell curls and alternate dumbbell curls are biceps mass exercises. The way I do my Scott Curls, they help my biceps peak. I do them upright so that my biceps are never able to relax. Consequently, this is a great peaking move. If you position yourself so that your arm is more horizontal, you'll work your brachialis more.

Concentration Curls are another great peaking movement. As I've said, my muscles are long, especially my biceps. It's harder for me to develop peak, and that's why I do Concentration Curls or Cable Curls.

How the Other Half Lives

Your other side of your upper arm is the "triplet" muscle. Your *tri*ceps has three anatomical heads and all three must be developed for the perfect triceps.

Again, variety is a key to success. Bench presses and other pressing movements will build nice inner or medial heads, but to get the long and lateral hards you have to do other movements.

I'm not as consciously aware of my triceps training weights as I am with my biceps. To me, the triceps is a "feel" muscle. I go for the pump and am not so concerned with poundages.

When I do Triceps Pushdowns with my elbows directed in, I put the workload on my inner or medial triceps heads. With my elbows out, I get my outer or lateral heads. Both forms of extensions, the Lying Triceps Extensions and Dumbbell Extensions, work the belly of my triceps—the long head. Finally, Triceps Kickbacks are a great cramping movement. By this I mean they cause the long head to contract "harder than hard." By placing my shoulder in relative extension backward, the triceps long head is less effective as an elbow joint extensor. Therefore, it tends to cramp as I do the movement and gives me a better ability to control the muscle. Which means I show more definition when I pose it.

You can tone skinny arms or reduce flabby arms. Or, if you want to go all the way, you can follow my routines and build Ms. Olympia arms.

MY CURRENT BICEPS ROUTINE

Exercise	Sets	Reps	Weight (lbs.)
Standing Barbell Curls	1	20	75
	1	10–12	85
	3	10–12	95–105
	1	20	75
Alternate Dumbbell Curls	1	20	30
	4	10–15	40–45
Scott Curls	4–5	10–12	70
Concentration Curls or Cable Curls	4	12–15	30

CONCENTRATION CURLS

Sit on the end of a bench and pick up a dumbbell with one hand. Bridging your upper arm against the inside of your leg and keeping your upper arm stationary, slowly curl the weight to your shoulder. Slowly lower the weight and repeat. While you curl, anchor yourself by using your free hand against the top of your alternate thigh. Repeat for both arms and always breathe normally.

CABLE CURLS

Face a built-in pulley weight stack. Grasp a curling handle and, with your elbow up and out slightly, slowly curl the handle to your shoulder. Use the same curling and lowering technique as you do with the Concentration Curl. Do all your reps with one arm and then repeat with your other arm.

MY TRICEPS ROUTINE

Exercise	Sets	Reps
Triceps Pushdowns (with elbows in)	3	10–15
Triceps Pushdowns (with elbows out)	3	15–20
Lying Triceps Extensions	3	12–15
Dumbbell Extensions	3	10–15
Triceps Kickbacks	3	15

DUMBBELL EXTENSIONS

Press a dumbbell overhead. Keeping your elbow stationary, lower the dumbbell down in back of your head as far as possible. Then, with the strength of your triceps alone, extend the weight back up to a straight-arm position. Repeat with your other arm. You can also do this with both arms together, using a heavier dumbbell. Breathe normally throughout the exercise.

MY TRICEPS ROUTINE

Exercise	Sets	Reps
Triceps Pushdowns (with elbows in)	3	10–15
Triceps Pushdowns (with elbows out)	3	15–20
Lying Triceps Extensions	3	12–15
Dumbbell Extensions	3	10–15
Triceps Kickbacks	3	15

TRICEPS KICKBACKS

Lean over and grasp a dumbbell or cable handle and bend your arm at the elbow. Keeping your elbow joint steady, straighten out your lower arm, lifting the weight back and up. Try not to move any other part of your arm except your lower arm, bending only at the elbow. Slowly lower the weight back to the bent-elbow position. Breathe normally throughout. Do all your repetitions with one arm before doing your repetitions with your other arm.

9
SEXY SHOULDERS

It's no secret that certain areas of our anatomy generate sexual conversations among males of the species. Our biceps and triceps might not catch the average guy's fancy, but wear a revealing dress and whoa, that's another story!

CAUTION, SOFT SHOULDERS AHEAD

Men find shoulders sexy, too. When I was in college, I couldn't help but notice all the guys who had stolen the "Caution, Soft Shoulder" road signs and placed them in their dorm windows. This was a popular way for all the guys to let their wishes be known!

I'll be the first to admit, as an athlete, I never concerned *myself* whether men did or did not find muscles sexy. To me, sexiness is an attitude. I never could figure out (and I think a lot of women can't) why or how men find certain women sexy. Whatever, as the

dorm windows prove, many men find women's shoulders sexy.

It seems to me that sexual images of what is and isn't desirable are largely *dictated* by Madison Avenue. When Cyndi Lauper first appeared, I don't think people even understood what she was wearing, let alone appreciated why she was dressing the way she did. But, what happened a few years later? Kids started dressing like her. Lately, Cyndi seems to be toning her wardrobe down a bit.

What about muscle chic? Many women new to bodybuilding will say to me, "Well, I don't want to get too muscular like a bodybuilder." Then, after they try it for a couple of months, they say, "How can I develop bigger muscles here and how can I thicken this muscle," etc. Values do change.

I'll give you another example. Take a look at fashion changes in men's and women's suits.

In the Fifties, men's suits were designed with built-in shoulder pads. The wide look was sexy. Today, women are wearing wide-

Shapely sexy shoulders are simply a result of hard, intelligent training.

Developing Shoulder Tone

Some well-meaning physiologists are convinced that women can't build shoulder muscles. They say we don't have the structure or hormones for it. Tell that to Mary Lou Retton as she catapults through space powered by deltoids of dynamite!

I know those physiologists aren't completely wrong, but I think they have assumed too much. We do have smaller wrists, elbows and shoulders. We do have less testosterone. The facts of life dictate no matter how hard we train, we'll never get deltoids like Lou "The Incredible Hulk" Ferrigno. However, you might get deltoids worthy of Ms. Olympia.

I've worked very hard to get my deltoids to their current level of muscle tone and shape. I'm still trying to improve them. Again, my arms are so long, I need larger than average deltoids to stand with my contemporaries.

When I started, I concentrated on Behind-the-Neck and Front Dumbbell Presses. These two exercises are best for developing shoulder muscle tone. And again, you don't need to do much to make your shoulders curvaceous. Simply doing two sets of 15 repetitions of each exercise three times a week will do the job.

Pressing exercises work every portion of your deltoid structure. Your deltoids have three heads: the middle (often erroneously called lateral), anterior (front), and posterior (rear). All three heads are strongly involved in any pressing motion. This is why Dumbbell Presses, Barbell Presses, Behind-the-Neck Presses, Bench Presses and Incline Presses are exercises all bodybuilders use.

Beginning bodybuilders should work hard on pressing exercises. As mentioned, toning requires only a couple of sets. If you really want to develop width and thickness you have to work very hard because your deltoids are one muscle group that doesn't grow easily!

shouldered jackets. Most men, on the other hand, wouldn't wear a coat like that worn by David Byrne of The Talking Heads.

If wide shoulders are in vogue, why shouldn't women design their own shoulder width through bodybuilding? Let's face it, not too many men like unfirm *or* skinny shoulders. Something in-between is nicer. That means most women need to tone up their shoulders.

BEGINNING AND INTERMEDIATE DELTOID EXERCISES

The most effective way a beginner can work her deltoids is to work them right after the chest. Chest training provides a good warm-up and mobilizes your shoulder joints for the work to come. Train your back and arms after your shoulders. Again, do a three-day-a-week program (Monday, Wednesday, and Friday).

To start with, you should do two or three sets of 10–15 repetitions of two exercises, Dumbbell Presses and Behind-the-Neck Presses.

After several months of this program, you and your shoulders should be ready for an intermediate program.

As an intermediate bodybuilder, you'll still want to add shoulder size, but you'll also want to add exercises to make sure your overall deltoid shape stays harmonious. The split system gives you time to add the necessary exercises. With a split system, you train your deltoids twice a week—Monday and Thursday, or Wednesday and Saturday, or Tuesday and Friday, or any way you can space two workouts with ample recovery time in between. Here's my recommended intermediate program:

INTERMEDIATE DELTOID ROUTINE
Monday and Thursday

Exercise	Sets	Reps
Behind-the-Neck Presses	3–4	10–15
Front Dumbbell Presses	2–3	10–15
Lateral Dumbbell Raises	2–3	10–15
Upright Rows	2	12–15

You should be able to train on a split system, four-times-a-week plan while still maintaining a regular nine-to-five job. This is why the split system is so popular with amateur bodybuilders with other commitments.

GOING FOR THE BIG TIME

I put my interior design career into suspended animation in 1983. I came to the decision that I could realize my bodybuilding potential only by working out every day. Later on I went to a daily double split—training two times a day. When I stopped my design job and made the move to a daily training program, that was when I considered myself an advanced bodybuilder.

For you, such might not be the case. You might consider yourself an advanced bodybuilder on a time-in-the-sport basis alone. However, my design job was so demanding I didn't make great bodybuilding progress until I stopped. I certainly don't recommend that you go out today and quit your job to be a great bodybuilder. Only the person who really enjoys the sport and has the actual potential to be very good should even consider such a major move. Otherwise, it's not worth it.

I do know this, no one has developed a great pair of deltoids without a lot of intense work. Deltoids are what I call "grit" muscles, the kind of muscles that are hard to develop. Usually they are endurance muscles and do not pump up easily. Some people have great shoulders naturally, and for others, no matter how much work you do, they don't grow!

BEGINNING DELTOID ROUTINE
Monday, Wednesday, and Friday

Exercise	Sets	Reps
Behind-the-Neck Presses	2–3	10–15
Front Dumbbell Presses	2	10–15

BEHIND-THE-NECK PRESSES

Sit on the end of a bench with a bar placed across your trapezius muscles behind your neck. Using a slightly wider than shoulder-width grip, press the bar to arm's length. Exhale as you press the bar up. Inhale, lower the bar back to your shoulders very slowly, and repeat. I suggest you wear a lifting belt to help stabilize your back during this exercise.

BEGINNING DELTOID ROUTINE
Monday, Wednesday, and Friday

Exercise	Sets	Reps
Behind-the-Neck Presses	2–3	10–15
Front Dumbbell Presses	2	10–15

DUMBBELL PRESSES

Standing or seated, hold a dumbbell in each hand at shoulder level. Push one dumbbell up to arm's length while holding the other one at your shoulder. Exhale as you press the dumbbell. Lower the dumbbell back down, inhaling as you do. After the dumbbell is back down, press the other dumbbell up, using the same breathing pattern. Alternate shoulder presses in this manner until you've completed all your repetitions. Never hold your breath and always wear a belt during this exercise. For better stabilization, you can sit against a bench or your training partner in back-to-back fashion to do Seated Dumbbell Presses.

One good thing about grit muscles, though, is they don't atrophy as much when you stop working them! What muscles do I consider grit muscles? Deltoids, forearms, calves, and neck. I've known many great bodybuilders who retain big calves even when they stop working them. The same is true with deltoids, although to a lesser extent. Compare this with the pectoralis major. A couple of months off and the muscle is half its former size!

Most bodybuilders find shoulders hard to develop. That's why I devote almost an entire session to my deltoids (I work my ab-dominals along with shoulders, too). In the past (and I still recommend it for most people), I trained my chest and deltoids together. Sometimes in the same session and sometimes one body part in the morning and one in the evening. Any pushing or pressing exercise invariably involves both your chest and deltoid muscles. If you train them both on the same day and then rest for three days, you ensure recovery for your next growth-producing workout. Only when your body has adapted to more severe workloads should you consider NOT working these muscle groups together.

Push-Pull

I'm at that point now. I train my chest and back on the same day. In the vernacular, this is called a "push-pull" system of training. I believe a push-pull double-split system of training is the most severe and advanced form possible. Why do bodybuilders do it?

I believe it produces a great volume pump. Back muscles are antagonistic (opposite) to chest muscles. Normally, as one muscle group contracts, its antagonist relaxes. However, it's hard for the antagonist to relax fully if it's partially pumped up and flushed with blood. Consequently, you never get full relaxation of your chest muscles when you work your back and vice versa, thus you work your muscles extra hard. I feel like "I get pumped through my body" when I do a push-pull training system. In one session I pump my pushing muscles. In the other session I pump my pulling muscles. One group of muscles never fully recovers before its antagonist set of muscles is worked. This is why I feel the pump through my *whole* body. I have made great progress the last year using this system. But, again this is an intense way to workout.

Sometimes I do 30 sets for my shoulders, but most of the time, between 20–25 sets. Compare this with a beginner's routine of five sets or an intermediate routine with 12 sets. When you multiply all that work by hundreds of training sessions, you'll understand that the deltoids have to respond. They have no other choice!

I use the full gamut of training methods to build my shoulders. This includes pyramiding and supersetting (actually tri-setting)! One of the things you discover after 5–6 years of bodybuilding is that gaining muscle size becomes increasingly difficult. As this develops, you cannot counteract it simply by spending more time working the body part or by lifting increasingly heavier weights.

In the first place, we all have limits on our time and energy. And, should you simply try to force heavier weights, not only will you overtrain, you'll likely get hurt. What you have to do at this point is find some way to make your training harder without using heavier weights or spending more time in the gym!

Tri-Setting to Delts of Gold

As I explained earlier, tri-setting is doing three exercises right in a row with no rest in between and then coming back and repeating the cycle. Doing one set of each of the three exercises constitutes one tri-set. Tri-setting gives me *stunormous* (that's a combination of stupendous and enormous) muscle pump. My current delt routine is on the following pages. I recommend it for other advanced bodybuilders.

My last three exercises are tri-sets. I do four or five tri-sets of these three movements. At the end of my session this is extremely difficult, but it makes my delts sprout like tulips in April.

I continue to make presses the base of my delt training. I add lateral and rear lateral movements to shape my middle and posterior deltoid heads. Upright Rows tie my front delts and trapezius muscles together. Occasionally, I do shrugs for more direct trap work. Not many, though. Women don't look good with traps like Lyle Alzado's!

Shoulders are a tough row to hoe, but you can do it if you work hard enough. Hopefully, women everywhere will appreciate that possessing shoulder shape can be sexy, too, and bodybuilders will understand that only through specialized routines can they mold deltoids of distinction.

ADVANCED SHOULDER ROUTINE
Wednesday and Sunday

Exercise	Sets	Reps	Weight (lbs.)
Dumbbell Presses	1	20	25
	1	15	35
	1	12	40
	2	10	45–50
	2	10	40–45
Behind-the-Neck Presses	1	20	75
Bent-Over Lateral Dumbbell Raises	4–5	10–15	
Standing Dumbbell Lateral Raises	4–5	10–15	
Upright Rows or Dumbbell Front Raises	4–5	10–15	

BENT-OVER LATERAL DUMBBELL RAISES

Bend over with your knees slightly bent and your back close to parallel with the floor. Pick up a dumbbell in each hand and raise the dumbbells simultaneously out to the sides until they are slightly higher than your body. Lower and repeat. Do not keep your arms perfectly straight; instead, let your elbows bend about 25 degrees as you perform your raises. Breathe naturally.

ADVANCED SHOULDER ROUTINE
Wednesday and Sunday

Exercise	Sets	Reps	Weight (lbs.)
Dumbbell Presses	1	20	25
	1	15	35
	1	12	40
	2	10	45–50
	2	10	40–45
Behind-the-Neck Presses	1	20	75
Bent-Over Lateral Dumbbell Raises	4–5	10–15	
Standing Dumbbell Lateral Raises	4–5	10–15	
Upright Rows or Dumbbell Front Raises	4–5	10–15	

STANDING DUMBBELL LATERAL RAISES

Stand erect holding one dumbbell in each hand in front of your body against your thighs. Lean slightly forward and raise both dumbbells simultaneously to a level even with the top of your head. Keep both your elbows and wrists slightly flexed as you raise the dumbbells and never let your hands get higher than your elbows as you make the lift. Breathe naturally.

ADVANCED SHOULDER ROUTINE
Wednesday and Sunday

Exercise	Sets	Reps	Weight (lbs.)
Dumbbell Presses	1	20	25
	1	15	35
	1	12	40
	2	10	45–50
	2	10	40–45
Behind-the-Neck Presses	1	20	75
Bent-Over Lateral Dumbbell Raises	4–5	10–15	
Standing Dumbbell Lateral Raises	4–5	10–15	
Upright Rows or Dumbbell Front Raises	4–5	10–15	

UPRIGHT ROWS

Stand erect with an overhand, pronated grip on the bar. Use a slightly narrower grip than your shoulder width. Pull the bar straight up, keeping it very close to your body and pulling your elbows toward the ceiling and slightly backward. Inhale as you pull the bar up and exhale as you lower the bar. Do not cheat by using your lower back muscles. You may find it beneficial to wear wrist straps while performing rows.

DUMBBELL FRONT RAISES

Stand erect holding one dumbbell in each hand resting against the fronts of your thighs. With a very slight elbow bend, raise one dumbbell up to shoulder height and return it slowly to the starting position, then proceed with the other dumbbell. Raise the dumbbells up in a frontal plane. Do not swing the weights up with your low back muscles. Inhale as you raise each dumbbell and exhale as you lower it.

10
BEAUTIFUL BACK

Paul Goode, an expert physique and fashion photographer, once wrote that I had the most beautiful back in bodybuilding. It's easy to see why Paul is considered an expert—at least by me! Naturally, I'm flattered. I've worked as hard on my back as any body part, so I feel pretty darn good when a man of Paul's stature comments on my back.

The back is an incredibly complex body part. There are more than 10 muscles that attach to your shoulder blade alone! You have to do a wide variety of exercises because of this. Otherwise, you'll never work each muscle in all the possible motions through which they contract.

Women aren't supposed to be able to develop wide backs. Indeed, you don't see many top women bodybuilders doing lat spreads. Most who try look a little anemic and not many can spread their lat muscles like the wings of Icarus.

Like Icarus, who spread his wings and soared too near the sun, I've boldly experimented with unusual back-building routines. Unlike Icarus, I know my limits. You

have to be careful with your back training. Too much, too often, and you might easily end up in traction!

BACK INJURY

Today, one out of five adults suffers from low back pain. Many of these people are hospitalized and eventually undergo back surgery. Many more people suffer transient bouts of back pain without registering official complaints about it.

Low back pain will cost the United States $81 million in 1987. Low back pain will continue to be the leading cause of worker disability, accounting for 25% of all insurance claims.

As I mentioned in my chapter on abdominals, weak, out-of-shape stomach muscles are a prime cause of low back pain and injury. The best way to prevent this is to practice a little bodybuilding medicine. Now, it's quite clear that some sports and recreational activities are bad for your back. Offensive football linemen, because of the techniques used for blocking opponents, often suffer low back pain and disc herniation. Competitive gymnasts, because of the forced arching of the lower back, also are prone to low back pain.

Powerlifters and Olympic-style weightlifters, who squat and deadlift repetitively with very heavy weights, suffer their share of back muscle pulls, but because of their strong abdominals and flexible leg muscles seldom experience disc problems. Recreational joggers often find themselves on the traction table. This is due to the repetitive pounding and compressive forces placed on their spinal ligaments and disc facets. It's a lot worse if the runner is overweight, wears lousy running shoes, and jogs across unfriendly terrain! If they're smart, bodybuilders *never* experience back pain.

Herman Goerner I'm Not!

Back in the early 1900's a South African strong man deadlifted 795 pounds with two hands and 723 pounds with one hand! His name was Herman Goerner. Herman had hands as big as Pete Rose's baseball mitt and his arms hung down from his shoulders to his knees. I mean this guy had some long arms! He was perfectly built for deadlifting.

Herman Goerner popularized deadlifting as an exercise for building phenomenal back strength. It is an elemental lift needing little technique. Today, the Deadlift is part of official powerlifting competition and is practiced by athletes everywhere to build strength. However, *unless* you have the mechanical leverage (long arms and a short back) to *avoid* injuring yourself when you perform a Deadlift, you should be very careful.

Since Goerner did nearly 800 pounds at the turn of the century, the record has gone up to 900 pounds, a feat recently performed by a 340-pound powerlifter from Oregon name Doyle Kenady.

Over that time span, though, many, many people have injured themselves deadlifting, myself included. To be a good deadlifter, but more importantly one built to avoid injuries when doing deadlifts, you should have a wide, thick waist, long arms, and a short torso. I don't have a wide waist and I don't have a short back, although I do have rather long arms.

When I started bodybuilding, I was also involved in track and strength activities. I did what the others did—deadlifted. And, I wasn't too bad at it. Before long I made over 300 pounds for three repetitions. Before long, I also injured myself, tearing muscles. I did poorly in the 1983 Nationals because I tore back muscles and couldn't train. I injured myself deadlifting and I don't plan on ever doing it again.

I'm convinced that heavy deadlifting should be left to powerlifters with good leverage. All other athletes, including bodybuilders, should be very cautious with Deadlifts.

You can still strengthen and condition your back muscles to help prevent injuries as you get older. Back pain is not just caused by weak abdominals. You may be predisposed to back problems structurally and not even know it. Tightness in the small, intrinsic muscles near your spine can cause muscle spasm upon exertion. This is another major cause of back pain. In general, weak back muscles may buckle under the strain of any heavy exertion.

The fact of the matter is, to completely avoid back pain, you need strong, flexible back muscles, as well as well-toned abdominal muscles.

HOW TO TONE UP TO STOP INJURY BEFORE IT STARTS

It doesn't take much to tone up your back muscles. Stretching isn't hard either. Bodybuilding and flexibility work just about guarantee that you'll *never* experience a bad back!

If you do 50 crunch-style Sit-Ups every day, in addition to 50 modified Floor Hyperextensions, and do a brief session of hip flexor, back extensor, and hip extensor stretches every other day, you'll probably stay free from back strain, provided you are not on your feet all day long and practice good mechanics if you are required to lift repetitively, heavy *or* light objects.

You already know how to do Crunches. For Floor Hyperextensions, lie prone, on your stomach, with your arms at your sides, then simply lift your head and shoulders and your legs toward the ceiling and hold this position for 10 seconds. Then relax and repeat five more times.

Alternatively, you can lift up as far as you can one time, come back down, take a one-second rest and repeat 49 more times.

After your Crunches and Hyperextensions, do stretches—10 for hamstrings, 10 for low back, and 10 for hip flexors. To stretch your hamstrings, simply sit with your legs spread apart about 30 inches. Then, lean your upper body out over one leg and hold this position for 10 seconds. Then, lean out over your other leg for 10 seconds. Do this stretch over each leg 10 times per leg. Remember to stretch slowly, until you feel tightness—but not pain.

Coincidentally, you will also be stretching your lower back muscles at the same time you stretch your hamstrings, killing two birds with one stone. To stretch your hip flexors (the muscles along the front of your thigh), simply sit down on your shins (lower legs tucked underneath you) and then gradually lean backward. As you get into an uncomfortable position, hold for 10 seconds, relax, and repeat. All told, these few simple exercises and stretches should not take more than 15–20 minutes a day. What's 15 minutes a day for a lifetime free from back pain?

The real trick to avoiding back pain is good body mechanics whenever you lift something. When you bend over to pick up a light object without bending your knees and using your big leg muscles, the force upon your spinal discs is multiplied some 10 times! In other words, if you bend over and pick up a 10-pound object with your legs straight, the theoretical force upon your lumbar discs is 100 pounds! So, whenever you pick up any object, always make sure you squat and lift with your leg muscles, not your back muscles.

A BACK CAST FROM BRONZE

Your back is a wonderful creation, full of majestically powerful muscles. Your erector spinae, which run up and down along the sides of your spine, are among the most powerful muscles in your body. Your latissimus dorsi, or "lats" for short, run all the way from the bottom of your low back and up along the sides of your back and go around and attach underneath your armpit to your upper arm bone. When developed to their max, they truly do take on the look of soaring eagles.

When you start bodybuilding, never neglect your back just because your eyes are located on the front side of your body! This is a crucial mistake many young bodybuilders make. They ignore their back. If you do so, it'll get you in the end.

I believe the two best back exercises for beginners are rowing and chinning. Beginners should do medium-to-wide grip Pull-Ups and some form of rowing. When bodybuilders say chins, they usually mean Pull-Ups. When you pull yourself up to a bar with your hands supinated (palms up), that's a Chin-Up and primarily works your biceps or arm flexor muscles. To build your back (even though your arm muscles are

unavoidably involved), do Pull-Ups with your hands pronated (palms turned away from you).

Medium-width Pull-Ups (with hands 24–30 inches apart) build your upper back muscles very well. Because an extreme stretch is placed on your lats and the lower part of your scapula rotates outward in the down position and then moves in and back as you pull up, the Pull-Up is a great exercise for isolating and widening your lats. As a beginner do two or three sets of Pull-Ups, for as many reps as you can do.

However, that may be a problem for some of you, if you are heavy or not strong enough to do Pull-Ups. If this is the case, do not despair. Instead of trying Pull-Ups, reverse the action, and do *Pulldowns* on a lat machine. This is essentially the same action as a Pull-Up, only reversed. As a beginner, start with three sets of 12 repetitions.

Doing a Lat Machine Pulldown and/or Pull-Up is an art. In either case, always keep your chest held high (expanded) and always concentrate on getting your elbows back and down *behind* your body. This is important in two positions: one, at the top end of your Pull-Up, and two, at the bottom end of your Pulldown. What you do is pull through, all the way, while your chest is expanded. In this way, your elbows end way behind your body. Your lats are responsible for extending your shoulder joint and that's precisely what happens in these two positions.

After doing 2–3 sets of either Pull-Ups or Pulldowns, go on to rows. I suggest you try Bent-Over Rows with a bar, but make sure you keep your knees bent and do *not* try to use heavy weights. This exercise may be too stressful to your lower back, even with good technique. If this proves to be the case, do your rows with a dumbbell, one hand at a time. As you row with one arm, keep your opposite knee and hand braced up on a bench. Do two sets of 12 repetitions on your rows.

Which Exercises to Add?

As you advance to intermediate training on the split system, with more time and energy to train, you must be careful to add the right back exercises to continue to make progress toward complete back development. Essentially, I've already given you a width exercise and a thickness exercise. In actuality, it's impossible to differentiate width-building from thickness-building because muscles responsible for both qualities are involved in every back exercise. However, a Pull-Up involves your lats as the prime mover, whereas a rowing motion puts more emphasis on your inner back muscles, such as your rhomboids. Consequently, an exercise involving mainly your lats is called a width movement and one involving more of your inner back muscles is called a thickness movement.

An intermediate bodybuilder should add one more thickness and one more width exercise to her back training program. For your additional width exercise, I recommend Lat Machine Pulldowns with a straight bar or V-handle, if you've been doing Pull-Ups, and—surprise—Pull-Ups if you've only been doing Lat Machine Pulldowns. You should be strong enough to do a few Pull-Ups now. If not, stay with the beginners' plan!

I'd add Long Pulley Rows for your new back thickness exercise. Long Pulley Rows will pick up your rhomboids, middle and lower trapezius, and teres muscles. You also need to add a specific low back exercise. You can do some moderately weighted Deadlifts (carefully) or Hyperextensions. Here's the way your new program looks.

BEGINNING BACK ROUTINE
Monday, Wednesday, and Friday

Exercise	Sets	Reps
Medium-Grip Pull-Ups	2–3	max.
Bent-Over Barbell Rows or Dumbbell Rows	2	12

BENT-OVER ROWS

When doing Dumbbell Rows, start with one hand and knee propped up on a bench while holding a dumbbell in your opposite hand. Keeping your back flat with your other knee slightly bent, pull the dumbbell from a fully stretched position up to your shoulder-chest junction. Hold for a second and lower slowly. Again, concentrate on driving your elbow up and back with the power of your upper back muscles. Inhale as you pull the weight up and exhale as you resist the weight coming down.

When doing Barbell Rows, grasp the bar with an overhand grip. Keep your back just slightly above parallel to the floor and maintain a 10–20-degree angle of knee flexion. This takes strain off your lower back. Grab the bar with a grip just slightly wider than your shoulder width and pull the bar up so that it touches your navel region. Get your elbows back behind your body, but do not yank the weights up. Concentrate on good form. Inhale as you raise the weight, exhale as you slowly lower the weight.

INTERMEDIATE BACK ROUTINE
Monday and Thursday

Exercise	Sets	Reps
Medium-Grip Pull-Ups	2–3	max.
Supported Bent-Over Rows	2–3	10–12
Lat Machine Pulldowns	2–3	10–15
Long Pulley Rows	2–3	10–15
Hyperextensions or Deadlifts (medium weight)	3	15

SUPPORTED BENT-OVER ROWS

You'll need a special apparatus for this exercise (or you can rig something together that'll suffice). Lie face down on a bench, angled at about 50 degrees with the floor. Stabilize yourself with your feet so that you don't lose your position. Grasp a handle with weights attached or simply use a barbell or dumbbells at arms' length. Pull the handles or weights up toward your chest as far as you can. Exhale as you pull the weight up, inhale as you slowly lower it. Concentrate on getting your elbows back as far as you can as you pull the weights up.

INTERMEDIATE BACK ROUTINE
Monday and Thursday

Exercise	Sets	Reps
Medium-Grip Pull-Ups	2–3	max.
Supported Bent-Over Rows	2–3	10–12
Lat Machine Pulldowns	2–3	10–15
Long Pulley Rows	2–3	10–15
Hyperextensions or Deadlifts (medium weight)	3	15

LONG PULLEY ROWS

Sit facing a pulley-weight system with your feet blocked. Lean forward and grasp the exercise handle. From a fully stretched position, pull the handle in toward your stomach. Keep your knees slightly bent and make sure you drive your elbows back as far as possible. Exhale as you pull the weight and inhale as it returns to the starting position. Do not sling the weights back with the power of your low back. This is dangerous and ineffective.

INTERMEDIATE BACK ROUTINE
Monday and Thursday

Exercise	Sets	Reps
Medium-Grip Pull-Ups	2–3	max.
Supported Bent-Over Rows	2–3	10–12
Lat Machine Pulldowns	2–3	10–15
Long Pulley Rows	2–3	10–15
Hyperextensions or Deadlifts (medium weight)	3	15

HYPEREXTENSIONS

Lie on a bench in a facedown position with your feet anchored and your upper body hanging free off the end of the apparatus. Lower your upper body all the way down and then raise it up just slightly above a parallel position. You may have your hands assisting by holding and pushing off from the sides of the apparatus, or you can fold your arms in front of your body or behind your head. Slowly lower yourself down and repeat. Do not force an up position any higher than shown in the picture. Breathe normally throughout the duration of the exercise.

THE FINAL SCULPTING

There's always a right method to follow. It'll do you little good to add any exercise to your back training if you don't do it right. I've discussed Pull-Ups and Lat Machine Pulldowns, but what about rowing motions?

In rowing, technique is critical. For example, I've told you when doing Bent-Over Rows that you should keep your knees bent. You should never jerk the weight up and you should always keep your back flat. When you pull the weight up, position is critical. If you pull the bar to your navel, you'll work your central and lower lats. Pulling the bar up to your breastbone places more emphasis on your inner, upper back muscles. I recommend that you do a couple of sets pulling to both positions.

Dumbbell Rows have essentially the same effect and they are *safer*. When you anchor your opposite knee and arm, you automatically take the strain off your lower back. Dumbbell Rows also allow you more muscle isolation, which is critical for growth.

When you perform Long Pulley Rows, two things are critical. One, get a good stretch at the start of the row and, two, get your elbows back behind your body at the end of the movement. Never heave the weight back, but instead pull the handle to your chest while concentrating on contracting your upper back muscles. If you heave the weights up (as if you're auditioning for the U.S. Olympic rowing team), you're liable to fall overboard with a back injury! Don't heave the weight! On another point, at the end of the movement, forcibly flex your upper back muscles in an isometric contraction. This little maneuver develops your ability to control your muscles. Better muscle control means faster growth.

Some bodybuilders like to use a V-handle for Long Pulley Rows, and some prefer a straight bar. My opinion is that when you use a mid-position (as you do with a V-handle) between pronation and supination, you work your biceps more. Studies show when your hand is pronated when pulling, less biceps is involved. However, individual preference is the key.

In an advanced back program, you can either keep the five basic exercises and do more sets with varying repetitions, or you have the option of adding new exercises. I think adding exercises is best because the back is such a complex area. As an advanced bodybuilder, combining your back with your biceps exercises works very well. You can work them in the same session or work back in one session (morning) and work your arms in the other (evening). Here's a workout I recommend.

ADVANCED BACK ROUTINE
Wednesday and Sunday

Exercise	Sets	Reps
Wide-Grip Pull-Ups	4	12
Barbell or Dumbbell Rows	4	10–15
Lat Machine Pulldowns to the Front	4	8–15
Long Pulley Rows	3	10–15
Lat Machine Pulldowns to the Rear	3	10–15
Hyperextensions	4	10–15

LAT PULLDOWNS TO THE REAR

Start in a seated position on a lat machine. The tops of your thighs should be anchored or someone should hold you down at the tops of your shoulders for stability. Reach up and grasp the bar with a medium-width overhand grip. Pull the bar down until it touches the back of your neck. Make sure to pull your elbows way down and back so your chest is elevated. You should exhale as you pull the weight down and inhale as you resist the weight going back.

ADVANCED BACK ROUTINE
Wednesday and Sunday

Exercise	Sets	Reps
Wide-Grip Pull-Ups	4	12
Barbell or Dumbbell Rows	4	10–15
Lat Machine Pulldowns to the Front	4	8–15
Long Pulley Rows	3	10–15
Lat Machine Pulldowns to the Rear	3	10–15
Hyperextensions	4	10–15

LAT PULLDOWNS TO THE FRONT

Utilize the same position as with lat pulldowns to the rear. Now, however, pull the bar down to the high point of the front of your chest, making sure that you keep your lower back arched slightly as you pull the bar down. Breathe the same way and use the same technique. You may also occasionally use a V-shaped handle for an alternative muscle congestion. As you use heavier and heavier weights, you may want to use wrist straps for a better grip on the bar.

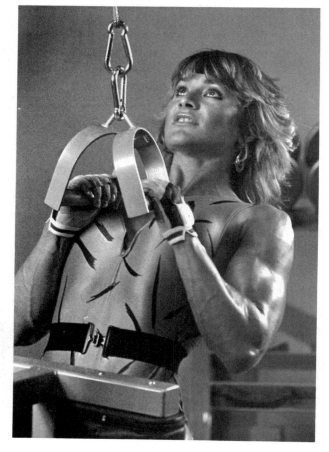

FROM A 727 TO A 747

I do six exercises for my back, with five sets of varying repetitions for each of those exercises. Thirty sets is a lot, but my back is well-conditioned and likes it!

There's nothing fancy to my back program. You don't have to get fancy—just work your back like you mean it. At present, I work my back on the same day as chest. I discussed why I do this in an earlier chapter, but basically it's an advanced "push-pull" workout that gives me a very thorough pump. My current training routine appears on this page.

Why do I do both Pulldowns to the front and to the back? Front Pulldowns really hit my lats. Rear Pulldowns narrow in on my lats, posterior delts, and scapular muscles. Sometimes I do these with a special bar that has handles on the end so that my palms face each other when I pull down. This attacks my muscles from still another angle. For my supported rows, I lie on a bench with built-in handles. Because my body is totally supported, I can concentrate fully on technique, isolating my lats to the maximum. You'll notice a lot of rowing in my back training. That's because I feel I have good width but still need to bring my inner back muscles up. I also like to do my lower back exercises on my leg day now. My opinion is that back training is one of the more

MY PERSONAL ADVANCED BACK ROUTINE
Monday and Friday P.M.

Exercise	Sets	Reps
Supported 45-Degree Bent-Over Rows with Bar or Dumbbells	1	30
	1	20
	1	15
	2	10
Long Pulley Rows	1	20
	1	15
	1	10
	1	8
	1	15
Lat Pulldowns to the Rear	5	10–15
Lat Pulldowns to the Front	1	20
	1	15
	3	8–12
One-Arm Dumbbell Rows or Bent-Over Barbell Rows	5	10–15

enjoyable body parts to train because it's so complex and you have such a wide option of exercises to choose from. Still, like any body part, you have to adjust your training to build up your weak sections. If you don't, you'll never fly. On the other hand, if you follow my advice you'll develop wings so fine you'll have no problem getting off the ground! You might even fly to the sun, like Icarus.

11
ENVIABLE LEGS

"Man-o-man, has she got a pair of wheels." I happened to be the centerpiece of that broken jargon. I don't mind an occasional off-the-cuff comment about my "wheels." I'm proud of my legs. I should be; I worked hard to develop them!

I'd be seriously amiss if I didn't begin a discussion on leg training with a footnote. As most of you are aware, a lot of women are dissatisfied with their legs (butt and hips included). Of all the prime areas in want of being trimmed and slimmed, legs top the list. I think leg toning and slimming is so important, I wrote a whole chapter on just that topic (see "Slim Thighs and Buttocks"). Losing fat and toning muscles involves good nutrition, but most importantly, it means you have to get off your "fatty acids" and do something!

Bodybuilders, although they do want to lose fat, are more concerned with the best and quickest ways to either gain leg muscle or define the muscle they already have. And that, my friends, is the purpose of *this* chapter!

MY HEAD START WAS A "HIND START"

My nickname is Boomer. It refers to a certain well-developed portion of my anatomy. I'll let you guess where. My well-endowed butt, calves, hamstrings, and thighs are not due just to bodybuilding. Not by a long shot. I know that my early gymnastics, swimming, and especially track did wonders for my legs. I had a head start and so did my hind end. Sprinting does miracles for your gluteus muscles.

Track gave my soleus muscles in the calves a head start, too. Curiously, most female bodybuilders have short, high calves, without good soleus development. The soleus is a postural muscle, involved when you run and jump.

Another muscle that is highly developed in sprinters, runners, and hurdlers is the hamstrings. I have thick hamstrings and had them *before* I started bodybuilding. So, if you want to develop good leg muscles, sprint and jump instead of jog (although jogging will develop your soleus to a certain extent).

While track athletes do have muscular legs (take a look at Valerie Brisco-Hooks, for example), track will not usually give the bodybuilder the *muscle size* she needs to be successful in competition. Besides which, many people *do not like* to run and jump! You can do a lot of 40–100 yard dashes, downhill sprints, and bounding up hills and you still might look underdeveloped on stage next to a champion bodybuilder.

The Soviet Connection

Back around 1972, the Russian and Eastern European communist satellite countries, really moved ahead of the rest of the world in Olympic-style weightlifting. Of course,

they had had an edge since the mid-Sixties, but moved way ahead in the Seventies. Our Midwestern farm boys were left baling hay.

When I met my future husband, Jeff, he was the national collegiate Olympic weight-lifting champion. The studious type, Jeff had already started to scour the Soviet system and apply it to his training. Jeff felt that the Soviets were far better at lifting big weights overhead, not because they were better athletes, but instead, because of two things, numbers and training techniques.

There are no professional football players in Russia. No Howie Longs or Mark Gastineaus. There are no powerlifters (those who compete in the Bench Press, Squat, and Deadlift) in Russia either. But there are a lot of hungry young boys who want to be government-sponsored Olympic lifters. Weightlifting is big news in Russia. If they

had Wheaties in Siberia, some trapezius-bulging Gennadi Ivanchenko, who could snatch 6,000 pounds, would have his picture on the box! Russia has a lot of weightlifters to choose from. You can be sure if our strongest young men were channeled off to weightlifting school instead of going into football, the big Red machine would be a lot smaller!

However, Russia's superiority is more than just numbers. Their weightlifters train two or three times a day. Before the U.S. fraternity discovered this in the mid-Seventies, this frequency in training was unheard of. Our school of thought was train hard, rest a day to recover, then go at it again.

The Russians understood the complexities of combining training volume, frequency, and intensity. They trained hard. So did we. However, they trained hard *more often*. Russian weightlifters start young and are progressively introduced to gradual increases in training load. They are forever coaxed along so they adapt to higher and higher workloads. This is the secret of their success.

We should've known. Decades ago, Johnny Weissmuller trained for the Olympics swimming one hour a day. Today's champion swimmers put in 5–6 hours a day in the pool! Why should bodybuilding be any different than swimming or weightlifting? To win the Mr. America title in 1950, you might have trained 90 minutes a day, three or four days a week. Not anymore.

Style

There was something else about the Soviet lifters that caught Jeff's discriminating eye. Not only were their thighs bigger than those of the American powerlifters, but they also had unusually good separation of their quadriceps. In fact, their legs would make bodybuilders proud. The thighs of some of their lighter lifters swelled out from their knees and then tapered back into their small hips. This gave them an illusion of having extremely small knees and narrow waists. Just the look that a bodybuilder would beg, borrow, and steal for! Why did

their Olympic lifters have much better looking thighs than our powerlifters?

For one thing, their thigh development had little to do with training intensity, since powerlifters are the world's strongest athletes and routinely used heavier poundages than the Russian Olympic lifters. The answer could be found in three words: style, frequency, and volume. The Russians worked their legs more often, did more work, and they did their lifts in a completely different way.

Closer analysis revealed that the Russians and Bulgarians grouped together specific lifts to make strength gains. On paper, their schedule looks like this:

Day One	A.M.:	Power Snatch
		Snatch Pull
		Back Squat
	P.M.:	Clean Pull
		Hyperextension
		Sit-Ups

Day Two	A.M.:	Squat Clean Technique
		Front Squat
	P.M.:	Jerks
		Hyperextension
		Sit-Ups

Day Three	A.M.:	Back Squat
		Snatch Technique
	P.M.:	Clean and Jerk

What became immediately obvious: Their lifters work their legs *every day*. Either they do some form of squatting or cleans or full snatches or jerks, all of which actively involve their legs. It might be heavy or light, direct or indirect, but the one thing it is, is *often*.

Equally important is the way they perform their Squats. The Russians like to squat deep with the bar positioned high on their back. They wear special shoes with built-in heels so they can squat with their backs perfectly straight, channeling the force of the load through their quadriceps. U.S. powerlifters carry the bar low on their backs. Doing so seems to emphasize their hips, low backs, and butt muscles instead of their quadriceps.

Sometimes, powerlifting world-record holders in the squat have little observable quadriceps at all. Therefore, I decided to put all this information to use in my training.

DON'T SAVE YOUR SQUATS FOR A RAINY DAY

People argue about Squats a lot. Some experts say you don't need them at all. If you work hard on Leg Extensions, Leg Curls, and Leg Presses, you can skip Squats, they say. Others partially agree, claiming that Squats build up your hip muscles, bulk your buttocks, and injure your back and knees. On the other side of the coin, many people say if you can only do one exercise, make sure it's the Squat!

Perhaps you can make reasonable gains without squatting. I have no doubt several bodybuilders have done so. However, if you can Squat, I suggest you do. After my episode with blood clots, I was not allowed to do Squats for quite a while. Believe me, I didn't make very good size gains until I resumed them. My legs seemed like they were better in 1979 when I was squatting heavily. When I couldn't squat, I worked hard trying Leg Extensions, Leg Curls, Leg Presses, and Lunges, but gained little size. My legs got defined and shapely, but no larger.

Don't ask me why. People say Squats are great because they are the only exercise where you lift your body weight at the same time you lift a barbell. Maybe so.

They also activate an enormous amount of muscle in a multiple joint movement. Maybe so.

They also make you suck up the wind if you do high repetitions, thereby stimulating your metabolism. Maybe so.

Everyone makes these claims. All I know is that Squats work!

Beginning Leg Routine

I'll tell you a little secret right from the start. If you aren't used to Squats and you go gung-ho right off, you'll be hard pressed to walk for the next five days. When you start, don't be like Tina Turner and explode into a frenzy. No, squat like Andy Williams sings "Moon River"—nice and easy. Don't use any

I flex my legs for the audience during my posing routine in 1986 Ms. Olympia.

allow you to squat with your back straight. Your feet should be about 12–24 inches apart with your feet turned out about half-way. This will unlock your hips, giving you better flexibility.

Descend slowly, under control, until you get to a position where your thighs are parallel to the floor, or a little lower. Do not pause, relax, or bounce out of the bottom. Squat down, with your back flat, under constant muscle tension. At the 90-degree position (thighs parallel to floor), simply reverse your power and come back up. Never round your back over; always keep it flat and straight. Concentrate on pushing up with leg power, not your back. When you squat, look straight ahead, neither up nor down. Never let your knees drift in as you squat. Concentrate on keeping your knees and feet pointed in the same direction at all times. Your breathing will come naturally, but breathe in when you descend and ex-hale as you rise.

I also suggest wearing a lifting belt and eventually, as you squat heavier, a light, protective knee wrap. Squatting technique is important, more so than for any other exercise. Don't push the weight too fast! Work on your technique until you master it, then proceed.

If you are a beginner, training three times a week, you will not be able to do a lot of Squats or leg work since you're going to be pretty bushed by the time you get to your legs.

If, in the first few weeks, you can no longer approach your workouts with zest, cut out one set of each of your leg exercises. Stay with the routine for at least six months, then advance to the intermediate plan.

weight when you start, just do 10 repetitions as if you were holding a bar. Do this three times. The next time you squat, you can use a 15–20-pound bar and do one or two sets of 10 controlled repetitions. The third work-out, do the same thing.

After one week, you'll be over any initial soreness and then you can start squatting with a little weight. When you squat, raise your heels on a two-inch board. This will

BEGINNING LEG ROUTINE
Monday, Wednesday, and Friday

Exercise	Sets	Reps
Squats	2–3	20
Leg Extensions	2	15
Lying Leg Curls	2	15
Standing Calf Raises	2	15

LYING LEG CURLS

Lie on a special apparatus, stomach down. Your knees and lower legs should be off the end of the bench with the pads behind your ankles and lower legs. Anchor yourself with your hands so you are in a stable position. Slowly curl your lower legs up as close as possible to your upper thighs and butt. Do not jerk the weight up or lift your hind-end off the bench. From the top position, lower the weight slowly and repeat. Exhale as you lower the weight, inhale as you raise the weight up.

BEGINNING LEG ROUTINE
Monday, Wednesday, and Friday

Exercise	Sets	Reps
Squats	2–3	20
Leg Extensions	2	15
Lying Leg Curls	2	15
Standing Calf Raises	2	15

[Note: Squats and Leg Extensions were described and illustrated on pages 57 and 59.]

STANDING CALF RAISES

Stand erect on a block with the pads of a standing calf machine braced squarely against your shoulders. Go up on your toes, pushing as high as possible. Then, slowly lower yourself into a maximally stretched position. Always try to keep your knees locked when you do your repetitions and don't use so much weight that you have to buckle, using your low back and thigh muscles to get the weight up. Work through a full range of motion. Breathe normally throughout the exercise.

INTERMEDIATE LEG ROUTINE

Now you'll be able to work your legs hard and long, twice a week. You'll make greater gains because you can do more sets and more exercises. Squatting will continue to be your key exercise—upright squatting, bar high on your back with your heels raised. Now you start recording your workouts (if you haven't already done so), and push yourself, both in the amount of weight you use and the number of repetitions and sets you do.

Which exercises should you add to your program? Leg Presses using a 45-degree machine, Lunges, and Seated Calf Raises (see Chapter 5, pages 58 and 60 for descriptions of these last two exercises) are the three I recommend. However, that's not all you do because you also should increase the number of sets you do of the other exercises, too.

A word about technique. Squat as before, emphasizing your thighs. With Leg Presses, do them on a 45-degree machine. This is better than using an inverted position machine. When you do presses lying on your back, with the weight directly over you, there's more likelihood of back injury. When you do your 45-Degree Leg Presses, vary your foot positions to place different emphasis on your muscles. Placing your feet high on the board works your upper hamstrings. With your legs low and your feet close together, you'll work your lower quadriceps better. Remember, however, that when adjusting to these positions adjust the machine handles so the resistance is removed—don't shift around with the resistance engaged.

When you lunge, make sure you step well out, stretching your upper hamstring and butt muscles. Drive back up with your quadriceps. I like to do all my repetitions with one leg before going to my other leg.

Lunges are especially good for toning up your gluteus medius on the side of your hips.

Seated Calf Raises are for your soleus, the long muscle underlying your thicker gastrocnemius calf muscle. They also work your gastrocnemius outer heads quite well. Do them after your Standing Calf Raises. On all your calf work, try varying your foot positions from toes in to toes out. Although the other functions of your gastrocnemius muscle are inversion and eversion (neither of which is affected by foot position), you may activate the gastrocnemius medial or lateral heads more or less by shifting your center of gravity and changing the line of pull of the muscle when you switch from toes in, out, or straight ahead.

Leg Extensions should be done slowly, with a slight pause at the top of your extension. I don't think you build a lot of size from extensions because it's a one-joint movement, with main involvement of the vastus medialis and lateralis at your knee. This exercise is a good muscle separator, though, creating a clean line between the two vasti muscles and the rectus femoris in the middle of your thigh.

Leg Curls are your main hamstring exercise. You'll need to work very hard on them to counterbalance all your quadriceps work. Lying Leg Curls are not meant to be done with really heavy weights. If you start lifting your seat off the bench, you are using too much weight and cheating by using your stronger back muscles. This is a shaping exercise, so go slow and concentrate on the action of your muscles, not the weight!

Some muscle groups respond to lower reps, some to much higher reps. I believe hamstrings, calves, forearms, and abdominals are high-rep muscles. Quadriceps, low back, upper back, triceps, and biceps seem to grow on middle-range repetitions. Your chest and shoulders grow well on low to medium reps.

INTERMEDIATE LEG ROUTINE
Wednesday and Saturday

Exercise	Sets	Reps
Squats	1	20
	1	15
	3–4	10–12
	1	20
45-Degree Leg Presses	1	20
	3	12–15
Leg Extensions	3	12–15
Lying Leg Curls	5	15–20
Lunges	4	12–15
Standing Calf Raises	4	15–25
Seated Calf Raises	4	15–20

45-DEGREE LEG PRESSES

Lie on your back with your shoulders up against pads. Your back should be flat or as close to flat as possible (several machines have a bend for your back in their lowest position; these are okay, but being totally flat is better). Position yourself so you are comfortable with your feet placed evenly on the foot board. Turn away the safety releases and slowly lower the weights down until your legs are almost fully bent. Without pause or rebounding away from the bottom, steadily press the weight back up, using your thigh muscles. Never jerk the weight or attempt to change your foot position while completing a repetition. Always return the safety catches before making any adjustments in form. When you have completed your repetitions, rehook the safety mechanisms. Exhale as you push the weight up and inhale as you lower the weights.

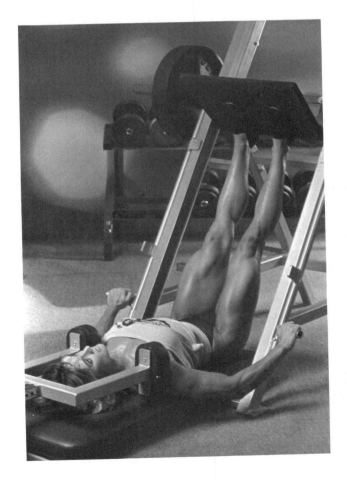

INTERMEDIATE LEG ROUTINE
Wednesday and Saturday

Exercise	Sets	Reps
Squats	1	20
	1	15
	3–4	10–12
	1	20
45-Degree Leg Presses	1	20
	3	12–15
Leg Extensions	3	12–15
Lying Leg Curls	5	15–20
Lunges	4	12–15
Standing Calf Raises	4	15–25
Seated Calf Raises	4	15–20

SEATED CALF RAISES

Assume a seated position with your feet on a block (actually only the balls of your feet are on the block) and resistance directed over the tops of your lower legs right above your knees. This can actually be weight plates, a barbell or pads on a specially constructed seated calf machine. Remove safety catches if you are using a machine that puts the resistance on your legs. Then, raise up on your toes as high as possible, hold for a second and slowly come back down into a fully stretched position, resisting slightly as you do. Make sure you go through a full range of motion and breathe normally.

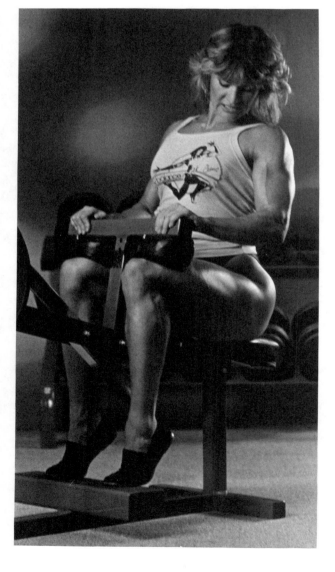

There's no reason you can't occasionally pre-exhaust your thighs by doing your Leg Extensions before your Squats, or supersetting your Leg Extensions and Curls. Variety is critical!

As a general rule, I recommend that you rest 60–90 seconds between sets. However, you may need longer than this when working your legs, especially if you are trying to push yourself through continuously heavy Squat workouts. The important point is that you get a good growth-enhancing pump in your leg muscles. If you are trying for more definition, naturally you should rest less between your sets. If you want more strength, you should try to recover more between sets so you can maintain using heavier weights.

LEGS THAT'LL TAKE YOU TO HEAVEN

Women bodybuilders often find that they can gain muscle size in their legs (with a good deal of effort), but when they try to define them, either they cannot or, when they do, they lose almost all their hard-earned muscle growth. In fact, women have a hard time getting cut in their legs, while they have no trouble doing so with their upper body.

You know by now that women carry much more body fat in their legs than men do. This makes it harder to gain definition but it can be done. To gain shape and muscularity, you have to do a wide variety of exercises and a lot of sets (surprise, surprise!).

There are no mystery exercises or magical routines that'll instantly add muscle to your legs. The best exercises are those presented in this chapter (and the earlier one on thighs and buttocks). As always, to maximize gains, you should use a holistic approach, utilizing different numbers of repetitions. Here's an advanced routine using a double-split system.

ADVANCED LEG ROUTINE
Tuesday and Saturday

Exercise	Sets	Reps
Squats	1	20
	1	15
	5	8–12
Hack Squats	4	8–12
Leg Presses	1	20
	1	15
	4	8–12
Leg Extensions	4	8–12
Lying Leg Curls	6	10–15

In the evening session, do your calf exercises.

You can see the differences in the total number of sets. The beginner does about nine sets; the intermediate, 30 sets; the advanced trainer, about 40 sets (don't forget to count 12 sets of calves in the evening session, four sets each of Donkey Calf Raises, Standing Calf Raises, and Seated Calf Raises).

When I train my legs, I divide the work up as quadriceps in the morning and hamstrings, calves, and low back in the evening. I've gone as high as 80 sets for legs, but most of the time I do about 55 sets over the whole day. Here's my current leg workout.

MS. OLYMPIA ADVANCED LEG ROUTINE
First Evening Session

Exercise	Sets	Reps
Lying Leg Curls	8	10–25
Standing Leg Curls	6	10–20
Donkey Calf Raises	4	15–25
Standing Calf Raises	4	15–25
Seated Calf Raises	3	15
Hyperextensions with 25–45 pounds added	4	15–20

DONKEY CALF RAISES

With this exercise, someone can either sit on your back or you can attach a special weighted apparatus around your waist. In either case, the resistance is directed through your hips to your calves. However, the partner, or the belted weight, should be situated back as far as possible. Stand up on a high block and raise up on your toes as high as possible. Hold for a second in the up position and then slowly stretch all the way down into the deepest heel-down position. Breathe normally throughout the exercise.

MS. OLYMPIA ADVANCED LEG ROUTINE
First Morning Session

Exercise	Sets	Reps	Weight (lbs.)
Squats	1	20	95
	1	15	135
	1	10	185
	1	10	215
	1	10	235
	1	10–15	250–270
	1	12	205
	1	20	135
Hack Squats	4–5	10–15	
45-Degree Leg Presses	1	20	
	1	15	
	4–5	10–15	
Leg Extensions	6	10–25	
Lunges	4	12–15	

HACK SQUATS

To do this properly, you need a special apparatus. Start in the top position with your shoulders underneath the pads and your hands on the turn-away handles. Position your feet so that they are comfortable and in the spot that you want them for the duration of the exercise. I suggest that you place them just as you would if you were going to do a Squat. Release the safety catches and slowly descend into a Squat position. Go down as shown, until the tops of your thighs are parallel to the floor. Do not bounce or relax in this down position. Instead, constantly flex or tighten your muscles to maintain good form. Slowly push yourself back upright, concentrating on your leg muscles. Exhale as you go up, inhale as you descend.

MS. OLYMPIA ADVANCED LEG ROUTINE
Second Morning Session

Exercise	Sets	Reps
Squats (using 135 pounds)	5	20
Leg Extensions	5	15–20
Smith Machine Squats	5	10–15
Hack Squats	4	10–15
Leg Extensions	3	20
Lunges	3	15–20

Squats and Leg Extensions are paired together in supersets, one right after another.

SMITH MACHINE SQUATS

Stand exactly as you would for a regular Squat except your feet should be closer together and placed in front of your body. Everything else is exactly the same. Smith machines have automatic built-in hooks that you flip on or off with your wrists at the start and finish of each repetition.

I don't really know what weights I use for the majority of my exercises. I go by feel and pump. I do keep track of my Squats, mostly for the fun of it. You'll notice I do a lot of pyramiding and I vary my repetitions considerably. I do a different workout on my second leg day.

I do my calf work either as part of tri-set or else just a superset of Donkeys and Standing Raises. Sometimes I skip the seated work since, as my soleus is well-developed, I prefer to concentrate on my gastrocnemius instead. I also like to work my low back on my leg day since leg work also works your low back. This is optional though. Many bodybuilders do all their back work on a separate day.

The heart of my Ms. Olympia leg workout is the Squat/Leg Extension superset. This is a volume muscle-congestion routine. The weight used is not too important. I just try to pump my thighs up. I do this only during the last three months before a show. Off-season, I just do a conventional squatting session.

The Smith Machine Squats are crucial, too. I stand with my body well in front of the Smith machine so I'm almost pushing backward as I make the lift. It's a great way to further isolate your quadriceps. You don't need to use much weight.

SECOND EVENING SESSION

Exercise	Sets	Reps
Standing Leg Curls	4–5	12–20
Lying Leg Curls	4–5	12–20
Donkey Calf Raises	4	15
Standing Calf Raises	4	15
Seated Calf Raises	4	15
Hyperextensions	4	12–20

I do my calf work either as part of tri-set or else just a superset of Donkeys and Standing Raises. Sometimes I skip the seated work since my soleus is well-developed and I prefer to concentrate on my gastrocnemius instead. I also like to work my low back on my leg day since leg work also works your low back. This is optional though. Many bodybuilders do all their back work on a separate day.

I do a few more sets of Leg Extensions near the end of this workout to flush my knees with blood after doing Smiths and Hacks, which put a lot of pressure on them. It also rewarms my knees for Lunges, another real bear on your knee joints.

I don't do any stair bounding or sprinting right now. I don't have the time for it, but if I did, you can bet you'd see me bounding about through the local parks once or twice a week. I still recommend a good hour-session of running and bounding for all beginners and intermediates looking for that extra edge in leg development.

They say that everything's on loan here on Earth—you can't take it with you. So, you can't bring your barbells to heaven. That being the case, you might as well try my leg routines. At least that way, you'll have such good legs when you enter your contests, it'll be like heaven on Earth when you accept your first-place trophy!

12
HEART AND SOUL

I love competition and I love to perform. It's the best kind of addiction a bodybuilder can have. My addiction runs deep, all the way to my soul.

I remember a dreamy Las Vegas night, when my husband, Jeff, and I stood on-stage, the proud American Couples champions. When we embraced that night, the thrill penetrated all the way through. I got the same wonderful vibes when I won the 1984 Nationals. Jeff and I cried like little children. My Ms. Olympia titles will also stay indelibly etched in my memory.

You might ask, "Well, who doesn't feel this way when they win?" Yes, winning makes life worthwhile, but somehow, bodybuilding's importance transcends winning and losing. I believe this.

The biggest thrill of bodybuilding is visual victory. You win on the day of your show *no matter where you place.* You've won because you've changed your body. You've become the shapely butterfly you sought to be. No one can take this from you. The final physical affirmation of your dreams and efforts is now yours and yours alone. It matters little how others judge it! You've given yourself and now it shows. Competition is the expression of a bodybuilder's heart and soul!

A SPORT IS A SPORT IS A SPORT

People still struggle to differentiate a bodybuilder from a weightlifter or powerlifter. Some people deny the existence of all three and refer to anyone who touches a barbell as a weight-trainer!

Even the National Strength Coaches Association seems confused. They tell youngsters to "strength train," but when they then recommend nothing less than 10 repetitions for safety, they mean "bodybuilding." *Strength training* is a misnomer as they are using it, since strength is built with heavy weights and low repetitions. What they should say instead is bodybuilding. But they won't, because they are afraid of the word and they don't understand what it means!

It's time I set your mind at ease.

Olympic weightlifting is practiced worldwide and champions are determined in the Olympic Games. More often than not, such weightlifters are represented by giant superheavyweights who waddle up to a 500-pound bar. Not all weightlifters are so ponderous and the majority of them move like quick, agile cats no matter what their size or weight. Weightlifters compete in two events, the Snatch and the Clean and Jerk. They see who can lift the most in these two events in specified weight divisions.

Powerlifting is a separate sport consisting of the Bench Press, Squat and Deadlift. Competitors also attempt to lift as much as they can in each event, with the highest aggregate winning in specified weight divisions.

Powerlifting and weightlifting both require skill. They are judged by consistent, objective rules. Consequently, whether you regard the activities as bizarre or not, it's easy to designate them as sports.

Bodybuilding isn't so simple. To my knowledge, bodybuilding is the only competitive activity where you do something *different* in competition than in training. Think about it. In bodybuilding competition you pose, but 90% of your preparation time is spent training—lifting bars and dumbbells. In basketball practice, you dribble and shoot baskets. This is the same thing you do in the game. The same relationship of practice to performance holds true for football, baseball, soccer, bowling, and every other sport. In bodybuilding competition you don't lift a thing. You just hope your training will lift you to first place!

Bodybuilding can be your sport, even if you don't compete. In fact, the large majority of people who say, "I'm a bodybuilder," have no intentions whatsoever of ever comparing their musculature onstage. So, in common jargon, bodybuilding means training to most people. And therein lies more confusion.

What Is Sport?

Most people can't decide if bodybuilding is art, sport, or both. Why is an activity classified as sport? Sports originated as a diversion. People "diverted" themselves from the trials and tribulations of mundane common life to lose themselves in fun, organized activity with their fellows. I suppose things have changed from this original idea. Sports are now differentiated from play and recreation and, sometimes, even from fun.

To me, sport involves both physical skill and competition. When you go outside and walk around the block, that isn't sport. But, when you walk a lot faster and race others in an organized event, that's race-walking

The fruits of hard, persistent training. Reigning Ms. Olympia three years running.

and it's a sport! Technically speaking, strolling down the sidewalk requires skill, too, but it's not the degree of skill involved in real sport.

Different sports have different skill requirements. Almost everyone can participate in bowling, billiards, or bodybuilding. However, not everyone can participate on the horizontal bar in gymnastics or fly off a 70-meter ski jump!

Some difficult skills require hours of practice. Jogging requires less skill than figure skating. Bodybuilding requires less skill than high diving or gymnastics. To my mind, everyone can learn to be a good bowler or billiards player. It just takes prac-

tice. The same cannot be said for some sports. Sports like sprinting, high-board diving, gymnastics, and the decathlon require certain God-given abilities. You will not be a good decathlon performer if you don't have natural coordination. You don't need to be a born athlete to be good at bodybuilding, however. It has some skill requirements, of course, but most people can master them.

This is not to say that everyone will be a good bodybuilder. Like all sports, bodybuilding demands certain physiological traits of the participants. When a bodybuilder poses, he or she exhibits agility and flexibility, but mostly muscle endurance.

Posing is really a sustained isometric exercise for two minutes combined with graceful isotonic movements. It's quite tiring, I know. I won't let anyone tell me that bodybuilding's not a sport.

How do bodybuilders compare with other athletes in speed, power, muscle endurance, and flexibility? We're near the top.

How strong is the golfer's chest? How explosive are the billiard player's thighs? How agile is the jockey? How fast is the bowler? How much muscle endurance does the outfielder have? How strong is the marathon runner? (Probably not very strong, since most of these individuals look like they'd be risking their lives walking in a strong wind.) One thing bodybuilders are and that's *in shape*! By all counts, bodybuilders are good athletes.

Competition must be assessed or judged objectively. This is what separates bodybuilding competition from a beauty or fitness contest. It's painfully obvious, though, that the mass media don't know what goes on during contest prejudging! Bodybuilders are compared and scored on a variety of objective qualities including shape, symmetry, muscle proportion, definition, and size. By strict definition, one is not placed in first "just because you look good." No, there are objective criteria.

I don't think judging bodybuilding is any more subjective than judging a gymnast's floor performance or an uneven parallel bars routine. And what about the final decision in a boxing match or competitive pairs skating performance? Judging all of these events involves some subjectivity, but, like bodybuilding, the scoring is primarily based on objective criteria.

THE JUDGMENT DAY

Come judgment day you'd better be perfect or you won't make the grade. Bodybuilders have to get religion, too! Looking good to a bodybuilder means more than being tight-skinned and fit. You need certain qualities to excel in bodybuilding competition.

When you examine great works of art, such as the Farnese Hercules, you'll see that muscular men are depicted with thick, broad waists. Even a lithe figure such as Michelangelo's David has a rather wide waistline in relation to his shoulders.

This is not so with modern bodybuilders. The much admired wasp-waist came into vogue when Mr. Everything, Steve Reeves, popped onto the scene. Reeves had shoulders measuring 56 inches around while his waist barely measured 31. In the bodybuilding community, a narrow waist and small hips are admired. Wide shoulders are important, too. But, these characteristics are somewhat unusual in women.

What does a bodybuilder—male or female—need to succeed in a contest? Symmetry is one judged quality. Muscle proportion and muscularity are two others. Posing presentation is still another facet of your competition score.

Symmetry and Proportion

People refer to symmetry and proportion without understanding what they mean. Symmetry means geometrical balance. You are considered symmetrical when your structure is in line with accepted body-building anatomy. That is to say, your shoulders are wide, your hips and waist narrow. Your arms and legs are the correct length relative to your torso, and from side to side and top to bottom your muscle proportion and development is equal.

Symmetry is mostly inherited. However, you can improve your symmetry by adding muscle or removing fat from certain areas. Let's say your shoulder width is average and your waist is broad because you carry excess fat along your sides. If you specialize on your deltoids, doing a lot of lateral raises, you'll add width. At the same time, if you do a lot of waist reducing and calorie burning exercises and eat correctly, you'll lose fat

from your waist. Thus, your shoulders will be broader relative to your waist and you'll have improved your symmetry.

Some insist that symmetry shouldn't be scored as heavily as muscularity. I disagree. Bodybuilding is about choosing the best body, not who has worked the hardest. You get no points for effort, only the finished product. This is the way it is in all sports. If I trained for 10 years as a sprinter and someone came right off the street and beat me, there wouldn't be a thing I could do about it. The results of training *and* natural ability are what matters. Symmetry is even more important for women than for men, because we are not able to develop as much muscularity as men.

The next quality, proportion, has to do with relative muscle development and balance. If you have thick, well-developed calves, but thin thighs, you lack proper proportion. If you have great quadriceps, but no hamstrings or buttocks; if your biceps are fully developed, but your triceps are not; if you have thick abdominals, but little latissimus development—you lack proper proportion.

Symmetry and proportion are definable qualities and the lack of either can't be excused by the phrase "Beauty is relative." In bodybuilding, perfection is not relative. Bodybuilding perfection, when you refer to symmetry and proportion, is exact.

Muscularity

Muscularity for the female bodybuilder does not mean big muscles. Furthermore, well-developed muscles aren't any good if they're covered by fat! Muscularity really means shapely, well-defined muscles. It means that your muscles have appropriate qualities that bodybuilders call density and hardness. Women can still have these muscular qualities, although not to the extent that men do.

Muscularity does not mean excessive muscle definition. Thin people usually have excessive definition and aren't healthy looking. Your muscles must be full and healthy looking. Muscularity does not mean excessive vascularity (veins popping out all over the place), either. It means that your muscles are shapely and well-toned with an appropriate amount of accompanying fat. Some fat is necessary. Nobody expects Ms. Olympia to look like a skinned chicken.

Posing

To most outsiders, posing is bodybuilding. To us insiders, training is bodybuilding and posing is something you do to show what you've accomplished in training! Nevertheless, posing is the expression of a bodybuilder's soul. It is the art form of the sport, the way to show all that you've perfected in the gym.

It can also make or break a bodybuilder. Posing is much more than the two-minute routine that the audience witnesses. In bodybuilding competition, much of the evaluation occurs in what's called the prejudging rounds. In prejudging, the judges compare and scrutinize all the contestants for strengths and weaknesses. We are called upon to do several *compulsory* poses to reveal our muscularity and proportion and several "relaxed" poses to reveal our overall appearance and symmetry. To my mind, as this is where the contest is largely won and lost, prejudging posing is even more important than your free routine.

Weight Classes—Such as They Are

In the prejudging all competitors gather to do preliminary battle. Because this is a long, arduous process, most of the bodybuilding hype is given to the finals, which may be run in the evening on the same day as the prejudging or the next day. But the prejudging is where both the competitors and judges do the yeoman's labor to determine the finalists.

Competition is divided into weight classes on the amateur level. There are usually four divisions called lightweight, middleweight, light heavyweight, and heavyweight. However, this has changed on the national level to just three weight classes: lightweights,

middleweights, and heavyweights. In the past, various weights have been used to define each class. This, though, constantly changes as more and more women compete. Since I like to eat, I'm a heavyweight!

As an amateur, I never worried much about weight classes. I always knew where I'd be. In the professional ranks, no one worries about weight classes, because there aren't any! That's right, we just line up and go at it, big ones against little ones, tall ones against short ones, heavy ones against light ones. I believe this is far more interesting to the fans but a lot more difficult for the judges!

ANATOMY OF A CONTEST

Bodybuilding competition is divided up into a round system. Here's the way it works for the professional women: In the prejudging all the competitors come out in a line-up. The judges now get an overall view of who's

After the muscularity round is finished all competitors leave the stage. A small break is allowed and then it's time for round two. In round two, symmetry and proportion are assessed. Each woman comes out and assumes four different positions upon command from the head judge. These relaxed positions are: facing front, right side, back to judges, and left side.

After each individual has appeared in the four relaxed stances, the judges bring the lineup out and again compare different competitors one-on-one for symmetry and proportion. Because different attributes are being assessed, a woman who was ranked first in the muscularity round could find herself ranked fifth in the symmetry and proportion round!

in shape and who's not. Then we file off stage.

Next, each competitor comes out and goes through a series of compulsory poses. These poses are as follows: double biceps pose facing the judges, side chest pose, back double biceps with one leg extended, side triceps pose with one leg back and a front abdominal pose with one leg extended and with arms overhead.

After this comes individual comparisons in groups of three. Out of the whole lineup each judge calls certain competitors forward to compare in whatever compulsory positions he or she wishes to see. For instance, the first judge may say, "I'd like numbers three, seven, and nine to step forward. Please do a side chest pose." This judge and the others then compare to see who is best. After various combinations of different competitors have hit all possible poses, the judges have an excellent idea of where to rank them, from first through last. This is how they judge the first round, called the muscularity round.

When the two rounds of prejudging are completed, the early competition is over. All that remains for the finals is the free posing round and that is judged separately, usually that same evening.

Free Posing

In the prejudging, judges wade through flash. They call out for a biceps shot and then they look. Whose are the best, whose are the biggest and best-formed? Whose are the most clearly defined? Are their biceps proportionate with each other? Are their biceps proportionate to their legs? They do this with each body part and competitor to ferret out deficiencies and strengths.

So what is the function of the free posing round? There's an old saying in bodybuilding, "If you can't show it, don't bother to grow it!" (Actually, it's not so old; I made it up!)

In bodybuilding, you must be able to tie everything together, both in muscle development and the way you show it. Some bodybuilders simply look like someone stuck pieces of muscle on them with glue. There isn't any harmony to their development. They are disproportionate.

The same can be true with posing. Some bodybuilders have quite a bit of muscle, but can't show it properly. This is what free posing is all about. It requires the ability to display your development to its best advantage.

Your posing routine should demonstrate coordinated muscular grace. It should be powerful. It should be vulnerable. It should synthesize form and function. What you hope to do is string together 20–30 original poses that highlight your strengths and hide your weaknesses. It must look effortless, but it demands a great deal of effort.

You should glide through your poses like an eagle in flight, smooth as silk, without a hitch or stumble. Your routine must become second nature, as if you were walking down the street without a care in the world.

To become free and fluid, you must practice in front of a mirror so that you can see where your arms, hands, and legs look most natural, while advantageously revealing your development. You also should pose in front of other people without mirrors so you don't rely solely on mirrors for feedback. People should watch without rose-colored glasses and tell you what looks good and what doesn't.

When the big moment comes, remember, you pose for the judges, not the audience. Therefore, pose without noticeable shaking or grimacing. Hold your poses so the judges can get a good look. Make sure you show muscle and don't just dance around without a purpose. Posing should be unique and functional. Without function, form doesn't mean much. You have to be able to show what you've done in the gym! So this is what you do in a contest, but the big problem is how to get ready for the contest.

CONQUERING YOUR BODY

Someone once said that getting there is all the fun. Obviously, he or she wasn't a bodybuilder because getting there ain't so hot! Once you've decided to enter a contest you must prepare yourself for every eventuality. Although the biggest things to worry about are intensified training and contest nutrition, there are other factors, too. These include skin preparation, hair preparation, posing routine, choice of posing music, the fit and color of your posing suit, and changes in your personal life.

If you are training hard and eating the way you are supposed to be eating, you should *never* be more than 7–12 pounds

over your projected best contest weight. If you resemble Dom DeLuise, you have a lot of work ahead of you before you even start to *think* about contests.

If you carry too much fat then you will have to spend time getting rid of it as well as concentrating on building muscle and correcting weak body parts.

As I've stated elsewhere, my philosophy is that it's better to work it off than diet it off! No one likes deprivation, and as an athlete, limiting my food is more of a deprivation than doing some more training. It's far easier to shed fat than it is to build muscle. Therefore, the bulk of your effort should go to building muscle, and to build muscle, you've got to eat!

As far as I'm concerned, if you already train hard you don't really need to change that part of your contest preparation. Admittedly, this is a different approach from other bodybuilders who advocate radical training changes before a contest. However, keep in mind that they are wrong and I am right!

You do not need to make wild changes in your training plan before a contest. All you need to do is to bust your buns as always, change a few exercises here and there to prevent mental staleness, and tighten up on your nutritional plan.

Dieting for Dollars

Years ago, some bodybuilders used to eat up 300 grams of protein a day as they prepared for a contest. They also used to eat fats, but no carbohydrates. Some successful men even used to go on a zero-carb diet! All this proves is that people can be a success in spite of themselves!

I don't think you can maintain proper training intensity if you don't consume enough carbohydrates. Carbohydrates and fat—not protein—provide most of our energy. Protein is, of course, necessary, but even bodybuilders don't need as much as they might think. When I'm preparing for a contest, about 65%–70% of my daily calories come from carbohydrates. Twenty percent of my calories probably consists of protein and the rest, usually 10%–15%, is fat.

I believe strongly in consuming a variety of foods for the best growth and energy production. This includes simple and complex carbohydrates from all kinds of fruit, vegetables, breads, cereals, and pasta. People simply refuse to believe that I don't eliminate certain foods before a contest, but the God's honest truth is that I don't. I continue to eat sweets right up to the day of my show, but I don't eat very many of them and I always expend plenty of calories if I do!

If you know bodybuilding, you know that the biggest problems bodybuilders face are keeping the muscle we have built up as we go into contest preparation and, while struggling to keep that muscle, "ripping up"

our bodies as much as possible, which means losing fat.

The reason bodybuilders tend to lose muscle before a show is that they have to curtail calories radically to lose fat and sharpen up. The moment they do that, they start losing energy. When you lose energy, you can't train hard, and when you can't train hard, you lose muscle. What's the solution? Eating and training as if you are still trying to gain solid muscle for competition! In other words, you should be lean enough to compete some four weeks before your show. You'll do better if you can actually *increase* your caloric consumption as you get closer to your show instead of having to decrease it.

Here is an example of my Ms. Olympia schedule of training and eating.

TWO MONTHS BEFORE THE CONTEST

7 A.M.:	Large bowl of oatmeal, one bagel. *Supplements:* 3 guarana capsules, 3 carnitine.
9–Noon:	Training (one body part and abdominals).
1 P.M.:	Large bowl of oatmeal, with 3–4 egg whites mixed in, two bagels. *Supplements:* Vitamin-mineral packet, 10 amino acid capsules, one 1000-mg Vitamin C.
2–4 P.M.:	Leisure, recreation or outside business (later on, posing).
4:30–6:30 P.M.:	Training (one body part and abdominals or calves).
7–8 P.M.:	Large tuna salad, extra tuna and vegetables.
8:30–9:30 P.M.:	Sunbed tanning or brief workout if I missed it earlier.
9:30–10:30 P.M.:	Business (usually I'll have a cookie or sweet during this period).
10:30 P.M.:	Bowl of oatmeal with 3–4 egg whites mixed in. *Supplements:* 3 carnitine, 3 lecithin, 1 calcium-iron tablet.
11 P.M.:	Bedtime.

I will continue with this plan almost all through the year, but beginning two months before the contest I emphasize my carbohydrates even more.

I don't make any other changes from the schedule on page 156 until one week before my show. Please realize that I do eat occasional fruits, drink some milk here and there, and consume a few other things now and then, but that is the basic plan I try to adhere to all year. As far as the supplements go, I'll use them for 4–10 weeks. I feel they are more effective this way. Besides, I can't stand swallowing pills all the time.

You can also substitute with this meal plan. You could eat fruit instead of oatmeal, or pasta instead of oatmeal, or turkey or chicken breasts instead of tuna. You can eat broiled fish whenever you like. It's just that I like the foods I list here. I don't eat red meat and I'm not crazy for fish. I'm not crazy for milk or alcohol of any kind, either.

My diet is instinctively high carbohydrate and low fat. What do I do different the last few days before my contest? The last week I eliminate all diet soft drinks and drink only distilled water. I stop using cereal sweeteners. I stop chewing gum. I continue eating all types of carbohydrates, but go for total elimination of fat. Most of all, I train to control my body water.

Let's face it, the last week before a show, you are not going to add any more muscle. What you want to do now is keep your body water under control. After I eat, I immediately don my sweat suit and ride a stationary bike for 30 minutes. I know I tend to put water back on, but this method allows me to keep it under check. I don't really restrict my water, though. I drink a lot of it to bring the carbohydrates into my muscles. I train and ride to try to control my subcutaneous water. I continue to train hard once a day. The other training session goes to posing.

During your last week, you must keep your energy up because you need to work on posing and this requires a lot of energy. You need to eat a lot of carbohydrates. This is why I *do not* believe in, nor recommend, carbohydrate depletion and/or loading diets. You don't need them. By now your

muscularity should be showing anyway because you've gradually lost fat, built muscle, and controlled your body water. If you continuously keep your muscles filled with glycogen by consuming carbs, you won't need these procedures. You won't be storing excess water because you exercise to sweat it off (and, of course, limit your salt intake). It's a neat, logical system and it's not complicated. The simpler you can keep your contest preparation, the better!

In fact, toward the big day you should concentrate more on carbohydrates and even forget about protein! Most competitors complain that they go flat the day of the show. Frankly, it's no wonder. Bodybuilders don't realize how many extra calories they burn due to pre-contest anxiety. With your training, posing, and worrying, you burn up a lot of energy.

I think you should consume as much

unrefined carbohydrates as you want the last week before a show. Yes, I know this is just *the opposite* of what most of you have heard elsewhere. Just keep in mind that I'm right. Like I said, if you work out hard and control your surface water, your muscles will be full and your skin tight. You'll be able to get a pump and look hard and healthy on stage. You'll have the energy to put life into your posing routine. You won't look like a hagged-out junkyard dog on stage.

Here's the way I eat the last week before competition: The first four days I have moderate protein, high carbohydrates, almost zero fat and continue hard training. Then the next three days my diet consists of low protein (essentially the small percentage of protein that occurs naturally in high-carbohydrate foods), high carbs, and almost zero fat. I take training very easy, mostly posing practice, and stationary biking for subcutaneous water control. On the day of the contest, I have an early morning carbohydrate meal (7–8 A.M.). I also continue to drink enough water.

Let me make another point clear. When I say "high-carbohydrates," this is not a license to pig out. All this means is that my daily caloric intake has a high proportion of carbohydrates. I'm still following a balanced-calorie diet in the sense that I'm actually consuming slightly fewer calories than I'm burning up.

In the 1985 Ms. Olympia, I weighed 146 pounds the day of the show. The heaviest I was all year before that show was 155 pounds. Two months before the show I weighed 152 pounds. One month later I weighed 148–150 pounds. During that last month I lost about a pound a week. This was not much of a shock to my system so I didn't lose too much muscle as I reduced my calories somewhat.

About 10 days before a show, I actually increase my calories a bit. This is to prevent muscle loss and to increase energy. I experience so much general anxiety that I go into a negative calorie burn before a show. In days long past when I continued to decrease

my calories as a show approached, it was not uncommon for me to drop 10 pounds the last two weeks before a show. Usually, all of it was muscle and I didn't get any more defined, just skinnier. It took me four years of experimentation to work my system out. The thing I want to stress the most is to keep eating your carbs, keep training hard, and control your subcutaneous water through exercise. These are the keys to getting ready.

PUMPING POTPOURRI!

Every bodybuilder worth his or her mettle will tell you that there's more to bodybuilding than dieting and training. If you're a man you have to shave and shave and shave some more. If you're a woman you've got to fuss and fiddle with your makeup and hair. And, I suppose that there are some women who have to shave and some men who worry about their makeup!

One of the biggest concerns for many bodybuilders is getting a nice tan. Why do you need a deep tan? White skin reflects light. When bodybuilders stand underneath posing lights, their definition can be washed away if they don't have a good tan.

I hate lying in the sun. It's boring. I don't believe it's very healthy either. I'll get some natural sun if I'm swimming or throwing a frisbee or goofing around in the sun. Otherwise I get my contest tan by other means.

If you do lie in the sun a lot, be careful not to burn. Not only does repeated sunburn predispose you to certain forms of skin cancer, but sunburn also causes water retention and this will be murder if it happens right before your show. Lying in the sun may dry your skin, so you'll have to use a good skin conditioner to keep your skin soft and supple.

You can use artificial tanning beds. Different beds have different bulbs, but most of them eliminate the ultraviolet rays that cause burning. They seem, based on preliminary data, to be safer than our favorite

star. To prepare for your contest, I suggest 20–30 tanning sessions. This will give you a great base.

A lot of competitors (myself included) use canthaxanthin before a contest. This is considered a safe food-coloring dye. If enough of it is ingested, it'll bond to your subcutaneous fat and color your skin. While it's not a real rich, dark tan, it does add considerably to getting a golden glow. I use canthaxanthin before a contest. Otherwise, I think it's unnecessary. If you take one capsule with each meal and another before bedtime over 20–30 days, you'll get a good golden color. That's all you'll need.

I also use a commercial skin-coloring dye known as Fast Tan. This is a combination of approved skin dyes and acetone. It does not contain any iodine so any chance of skin allergy is significantly reduced. Almost all the bodybuilders in-the-know use this as nothing compares to it in producing a dark color. Other products are also used, such as Coppertone Sudden Tan and QT.

Contest Attire and Accompaniment

I make my own posing suits and have my posing music scored by a professional taping artist. You need a suit top that stays in place and covers your breasts. However, it can't be so tight that it threatens to explode if you move in the wrong direction. Suits usually need to be customized or made by a company specializing in outfitting bodybuilders. After all, we have different proportions than most women and swimwear manufacturers make their suits for a composite woman, not a bodybuilder.

The bottom of your suit should be cut to compliment your feminine structure. It shouldn't be square across your abdomen, but should be cut lower in the middle and extend upward at your hips. It also needs to be specially cut in the back to show just enough butt, but not too much. Like the guy who liked the electric razor so much he bought the company, I make my own suits.

Because suit fit is so important, my Corinna collection is customized for bodybuilders.

Color selection can be crucial, too. Most women today prefer the ciré wet-look suits, rather than the duller cotton standard. Wet-look colors, in brilliant orange, green, or lavender, can really bedazzle an audience, but you must pick a color that augments your tan and structure.

Women with long waistlines shouldn't wear really low-cut suits because they make the torso look even longer. Women with heavy hips should wear dark suits since light-colored suits make you look heavier.

Music is another aspect of bodybuilding. I think musical selection is much more important than people realize. You can see the fans come alive when a good piece of music comes on. Although classical music is stirring, it has too many places where the music abruptly goes melodramatic and soft rather than staying powerful and upbeat. I'm not sure the audience is sophisticated enough to realize that classical music tells a story, just as a good posing routine does. Classical music is beyond the appreciation of the average bodybuilding fan, so I recommend against it. Listen to it before you train instead! That'll get you psyched up.

Jazz is okay and if you get into a jazzy sound, you'll probably get a good response to it. Don't pick a pop song that's been played to death on the radio. No one will respond to it. Pick a somewhat recognizable piece, one that creates pleasant thoughts in people's heads. It should be dramatic with a rhythm such that you can hit powerful physique shots to the beat. Whatever you choose, you must use your music. Don't just be a zombie as if there's no music there. Spend at least an hour a day working with your music. And, for heaven's sake, record it at the beginning of a blank tape. While you're at it, make three copies.

Remember, you are a woman and you have to keep in mind you might get your period at contest time. If you are extremely lucky, your flow will start right when it's time to do your routine. Believe me, knowing how emotional changes can either in-

duce or stop periods, you better be prepared in case this happens!

Actually, I had my period the week before the 1985 Ms. Olympia and I know at least two other competitors who did as well. When you get your period, not only do you tend to hold water, but sometimes, you feel down and irritable. Understand what's happening and take steps to alleviate possible problems. If you seem to be holding water, hop on your stationary bike with a couple of sweat shirts on. If you don't have enough energy for that, take a relaxing sauna or whirlpool. In either case, you'll lose water.

If you get chocolate or carbohydrate cravings, eat the right kind of carbs. Don't stuff yourself with Hostess Twinkies. Eat bran muffins or rice cakes and pasta. You'll get satisfying, nutritious calories and won't have such a strong desire to bloat out.

One more thing—if you have a tendency for heavy flow and you get your period the same day that you pose, don't forget to bring a dark suit.

Skin and Hair

I make special efforts to take care of my skin. Some competitors do not and consequently their skin looks harsh and weather-beaten. You have to remember, lying in the sun and perspiring a lot can damage your skin. If you sweat a lot, you'll need to shower more often and this dries out your skin.

Nice skin is an important factor in beauty and competition. I recommend that you use a special skin oil after every shower, especially the last two months before competition. You should shower rather than take a bath, and do so in lukewarm and not hot water. Commercial soap will dry your skin even more, so only use it in places where perspiration reacts with skin bacteria. This includes your face, armpits, genitals, feet, breasts, and hands. As soon as you get out of the shower, put on a nice skin oil.

You'll find that a few of the commercial tanning dyes also dry your skin. Therefore, not only should you use oils after you

shower, but one hour after applying these skin dyes you also should rub on a coat of oil. If you want your hands to remain baby soft, use special training gloves. Then you won't have to worry about calluses.

Salt, grime from bench tops, and the sun will damage your hair, too, unless you take special preventive steps. Like teeth and health, your hair is a precious commodity, so take care of it.

Commercial shampoos are mostly the same, mixtures of alkaline soaps and detergents. Most of them are quite mild so it's okay to shampoo every day. Shampoo removes dirt and salty debris while conditioners build "hair body" by coating each hair shaft with a protective protein layer. Always apply a conditioner after shampooing. Avoid wave agents, hair dyes, or straighteners, as they do nothing but damage your hair. Although you'll do it for your competition, don't get in a habit of blow-drying your hair or saturating it with goopy hair sprays.

Neither does anything good for your hair.

I trust that you now understand that getting ready for a contest is a complete physical process from top to bottom. There are emotional and psychological preparations, too.

MIND OVER MATTER

I'll be frank, bodybuilding can be very hard on personal relationships. It requires a lot of time, energy, effort, and discipline. A lot of times, the bodybuilder's efforts are not matched by the rewards, so it makes it even harder on the uninitiated.

I don't know what's worse—a male and female bodybuilder who live together and want to compete at the same time, or one spouse who competes and the other who doesn't.

The advantage of both being bodybuilders means that you both know what the other goes through. You both appreciate the discipline of diet and training. Unfortunately, if you both have to train and diet, you both can become irritable and tired. Who will carry the slack in your private and business lives? If you have children, who'll attend to their very special needs?

Many bodybuilding couples I know who have jobs and family don't compete at the same time because it's really quite difficult. Jeff and I did it for a while, but we didn't have children and I was still a student or recent graduate then. Besides which, Jeff has the patience of a monk. Most people don't and that makes everything harder.

You'll have to understand *ahead of time* the tenseness and irritability that may crop up. Then take steps to head it off before it starts. Plan everything out carefully so you have time for yourself and for your loved ones. It takes special concentration to stay with a tough training routine when you are following a special eating plan and trying to cram 9,000 things into a 24-hour day that speeds by too quickly.

Many successful bodybuilders have

spouses or sweethearts who aren't competitive bodybuilders. This relationship also has its pluses and minuses. The mate who is not competing has to do a lot of things for the one who is. Maybe special meal preparation is involved, or special attention to children or job is required. Maybe there is little time for personal, fun activities. All this takes its toll and you must be aware of this and guard against it. Make sure that you and your mate resolve to be of strong mind. If you have that, you'll achieve mind over matter on *all* matters!

As I said earlier, bodybuilding is all about winning over yourself. It's not always about beating someone in competition. If you have what it takes to win over yourself, you'll be able to digest everything I've told you. If you can do that, you're on your way to all kinds of victories!

13
QUESTIONS AND ANSWERS

Q: *I'm 5'10" and weigh 119 pounds. I eat a lot, but I don't gain any weight. Should I increase my calories even more, and if I do, won't that destroy my symmetry and definition?*

A: As I've pointed out throughout this book, gaining size is not easy. You may have an overactive thyroid gland, but if you did, you probably would show signs of this, like profuse sweating and weight loss.

People have different metabolic rates, some fast, some slow. The thyroid gland governs metabolic rate. Your metabolism is fast, but it's probably still within the normal range. However, you can check this with your doctor and he or she can prescribe medicine if necessary.

To gain solid muscle you should sharply curtail all outside physical activities to conserve calories. Never walk when you can ride and never stand when you can sit! Lift heavy weights three times a week, working in the 8–15 repetitions per set range. Work on the Bench Press, Squat, Lat Machine Pulldown, Standing or Seated Press, Curls,

Bent-Over Row with bar or dumbbells, and Sit-Ups. When I suggest heavy weights, I want you to use weights that you can lift safely, with good form.

You need a lot of calories to gain weight. If you eat like a sparrow, you'll never look like an eagle. Do not eat all your food at one or two meals. Instead, eat 5–6 small meals per day and divide your calories over all these meals. Drink a lot of whole milk, too. It's easier to ingest a lot of calories through liquid nutrition.

Because you may have a fast metabolism, it will be difficult for you to add fat to your frame, so you need not worry too much about this. You are lucky in that you can eat a lot of high-calorie foods without gaining fat. Besides drinking a lot of milk (you might mix in a protein supplement, too), eat red meat, fresh fruits, complex starches (pasta and potatoes), whole-grain cereals, peanut butter, salads, and fruit juices.

I wouldn't worry right now about your symmetry and definition, because weight gain is your prime concern. An appropriate weight for a bodybuilder of your height is between 130–155 pounds. Actually, many overweight women would love to have your problem! I know how much you want to fill out with some muscle, but it does take time, so please be patient. Hang in there and good eating!

Q: *I get fatigued quickly when I work out. Is this normal? Am I overtraining? How do I know when I'm doing too much and overtraining?*

A: If you start training and 15 minutes into it you poop out, something's not kosher. It's normal to get tired, but not this fast. Chances are you aren't eating enough high-energy carbohydrates. Or, you could have a low blood sugar condition. To determine that, visit your doctor for serial blood sugar readings.

If you check out medically, look for other causes of your lethargy.

You should always leave the gym pleasantly refreshed. You shouldn't have to drag yourself out! Congestion and local fatigue in your muscles are normal. In fact, if you don't feel some local muscle fatigue, you didn't do enough.

Overtraining? This is one of the most difficult conditions to diagnose. If you feel tired all the time, if you do not look forward to your training, if you have a poor attitude and sore muscles all the time, you are probably doing too much. A more scientific way to tell if you are overtraining is to take your pulse every day upon awakening. If, on a morning following a workout, it's more than 10 beats above average, you may be overtraining. As you get used to training, you'll be able to do more and more.

To avoid overtraining, cut back on the number of sets and exercises you do. Cut back on the amount of weight you use, too. Switch gyms and get a workout partner in tune to you! Get plenty of rest and sleep. Eat a good supply of natural, unrefined carbohydrates, concentrating on fresh fruits and pasta. All these things should help you pull out of your training rut and continue progressing.

Q: *I'm diabetic and take insulin. I developed diabetes when I was 15 and am 22 now. Can I bodybuild? Will I get anything out of it?*

A: The first thing you should do is consult a doctor knowledgeable in both exercise and diabetes. There are plenty of diabetics in bodybuilding, including Mr. America—Tim Belknap.

The American Diabetic Association recommends exercise for diabetics. Exercise actually works like insulin by helping to move blood sugar into your working muscle cells. Since diabetics either don't produce enough insulin, or the insulin that they do produce is less effective than normal, they benefit from exercise. In fact, some diabetics can control their blood sugar through exercise and diet and don't need insulin at all!

What you'll have to learn is how to balance exercise with your need for insulin. Since exercise moves sugar out of your blood into your muscles, you're liable to need less insulin than before. If you take your usual dose of insulin and then work out, you may then have too much insulin and lapse into insulin shock. On the other hand, if you don't get enough insulin you can go into an insulin coma! There is a delicate balance. This is why you need your doctor's supervision.

Never overeat with diabetes. Eat a low-fat, balanced diet with adequate protein and natural, unrefined carbohydrates. It's healthier to avoid sweets, tobacco, and alcohol, too. Drink plenty of fresh water and ask your doctor if any vitamin or mineral might help.

Q: *My boyfriend is preparing for a contest. He's acting weird, irritable, aggressive, and he has no patience. He also acts like a sex fiend. What's going on? This is not like the guy I used to know.*

A: I've heard these complaints before. The winning physique standard for men is difficult to reach. The men must be large and

ripped at the same time. This makes dieting extremely difficult. For you and him!

All these actions can be the result of his hard training and severe dieting. At least, everything except his sexual antics! Maybe you should ask him if he's using anabolic steroids, particularly testosterone. Testosterone has been known to make male bodybuilders more sexual. Some experts insist that it also makes men more aggressive.

I'd suggest waiting until after his show before you force a confrontation on his actions. I know this will be difficult, but hey—it's part of what we do for our loved ones, right? Seriously, he needs your support right now. He needs to be confident. If his behavior suddenly reverses itself after the show, then you'll know it was his severe training and dieting. If he doesn't let up or change, he may be fooling around with steroids.

At that point you may wish to seek counseling. You will have to determine if his actions are a psychological-emotional reaction or a purely physiological reaction. Steroids do induce physiological changes in people. Good luck.

Q: *A year ago I ruptured a muscle in my upper chest. Now I have a big lump there. It's not painful, but it's tight. What did I do? Is there any way to get rid of it?*

A: Chances are you tore part of your upper pectoralis major chest muscle. It's probably healed itself by now—but probably incorrectly. Most of these injuries demand immediate intervention by a physician or they won't heal successfully. You should certainly see a surgeon, although he or she would probably advise against surgical repair now, since so much time has elapsed.

Your body heals injuries by laying down scar tissue as it repairs itself. To ensure that your new tissue forms in the same direction as your existing tissue, you need to do a lot of gentle stretching. Otherwise, the injury remains tight or painful.

You should visit a sports therapist. My husband Jeff is a physical therapist and here are his recommendations:

1. Before training, apply a hot pack to the injured area. Heat the whole area for 15–20 minutes.
2. After heating, do a variety of stretching motions.
3. Warm up well and follow with your workout, stressing full-range, high-repetition exercises. This will get more blood to your injured area.
4. After your workout, massage the area.
5. Following the massage, use an ice pack over the area for about 10 minutes. This will prevent any local inflammation, which tends to make the muscle tighter yet.
6. These procedures should be done every day!

Keep in mind that your injury is old and that you may never attain complete muscle recovery or function. However, all these procedures should improve the injured area.

Q: *I lost a lot of weight—90 pounds to be exact! I shed this fat in six months, but now I have loose skin on the back of my arms, around my thighs and hips, and on my lower abdomen. Everywhere else, I've tightened up! My doctor says there's nothing I can do about it, just don't gain weight again. Is my condition hopeless or can I do something about it?*

A: You lost a lot of weight in a very short time period. The recommended way to lose weight is no more than one pound a week. You lost, on the average, almost four pounds per week! When you lose this much weight so fast, you're bound to have some loose skin left over, especially if you were really obese to begin with.

The loss of skin elasticity is proportional to the amount of weight you lost, the time you lost it in and how much fat you carried in the first place. Your age and general physical condition are also factors. In other words, if your skin was overstretched for a long time, it's unlikely that your full elasticity will completely return.

Which is not to say that something can't be done about it! Your skin will tighten up

to a certain extent. A good bodybuilding program will help because enhanced muscle tone, which supplies skin pressure from underneath, will push your skin out better. Follow the advice for beginners in this book and maintain a program of aerobics, too. Eventually the exercise will help, but don't expect miracles right away. Give it at least as long as it took you to lose the weight in the first place.

Pay extra attention to your diet. In an attempt to lose weight too fast, many people erroneously lower their protein too much. Your body then feeds off its own muscle to supply protein. Since one of the main constituents of skin is protein, taking protein from the skin lets the skin deteriorate. You lose natural elasticity. From now on get at least one gram of protein per day for each kilogram (2.2 pounds) of your body weight.

If you maintain a low-calorie diet, make sure you get enough vitamins and minerals, which are vital for your skin's tone and integrity. You should supplement your diet with minerals and Vitamins A, C, E, and B complex. Keep your dietary fat low, drink a lot of water and train hard. If there's no improvement in six months, I'd visit a plastic surgeon. He or she might be able to remove some of the loose skin.

Q: *Have female bodybuilders reached their ultimate development? Can the current crop of champions improve or have we reached our genetic potential?*

A: I haven't reached mine! Life is progress. If you look in bodybuilding magazines of 10 years ago, you'll notice that today's bodybuilders are much better.

Better athletes are bodybuilding today. As the genetic pool enlarges, better bodybuilders will emerge and surge to the forefront. I do believe that natural muscle size in women is hormonally limited. If steroid drugs are legislated out of bodybuilding, overall muscle size may be limited and the rate of change in physique development may be slowed.

Drugs have been a factor in increased size

in some cases, but I think steroids are over-emphasized. They do little for symmetry or shape. They age your skin and destroy natural feminine lines by adding bulk where women normally don't carry so much bulk (the front shoulders and thick abdominal muscles are two examples).

I do believe that women bodybuilders will get larger. At the same time, though, I suspect the main changes will be better shape, muscle proportion, and symmetry, rather than muscle size.

Bodybuilders train harder and longer today. Equipment is better. Methodology is better. My book is available! There are greater rewards associated with bodybuilding today, so the incentive to go into the sport is greater.

Another factor is nutrition, including supplementation. Today's female bodybuilders know how to eat and use supplements better than those in the past. No longer do we follow low-carbohydrate diets or starve ourselves before a show. Back in 1980, I thought the best way to prepare for a show was to cut back my calories drastically, load up on protein, and exercise aerobically until I dropped. Such irrational and unscientific training nearly killed me when I developed a blot clot in 1981. I'm convinced my diet and training stress were the reason why.

We know today that carbohydrates are where it's at. Vitamins and minerals are more important when you restrict calories and increase sweat loss through activity. All these things contribute to the elevation of the bodybuilder.

I think the standard will continue to go up. I don't think we are close to our true potential yet!

Q: *I read in a newspaper that weightlifting was bad for my heart and that compared to aerobics, bodybuilding is useless. The article went on to say that bodybuilding would raise my blood pressure. Is this true?*

A: That newspaper is raising my blood pressure! The person who wrote the article is twisting certain facts. In the first place, bodybuilding is not the same thing as weightlifting. Weightlifters attempt to lift as much as they can over their heads in a one-repetition maximum effort. This type of lifting does not condition your heart as well as aerobics, but there is absolutely *no* evidence that it's bad for your heart, provided your heart is healthy to begin with.

When you lift a heavy weight one time your blood pressure does go up. But it also comes back down when you stop. What happens when you lift a heavy weight one time? As your muscles contract they put pressure against your blood vessels. This means that your heart has to beat more forcefully to move blood around your body. Therefore, your blood pressure goes up. But, as the pressure inside your vessels increases, so also does the pressure outside your blood vessels within the muscle. Therefore, no pressure gradient develops and this temporary increase in blood pressure does no damage.

When you stop lifting the situation reverts back to normal. The effect of lifting a heavy weight on your heart and blood pressure is neutral. It's neither bad nor good. If you have heart problems or high blood pressure to begin with, though, you wouldn't want to exercise in this manner.

You should do an easier form of activity, however, one that stresses large muscle groups from all over your body. Heart patients are advised to walk, swim, or do stationary biking for this reason.

With bodybuilding, of course, you do multiple sets and repetitions with lighter weights so blood is moved freely all around your body. Bodybuil high exerc

Th good ing, a do pr cle e increa the lor to-fat tion, y aerobi

Q: *How do you all year? All you all the time. Not ever California, so how do*

© Trix Rosen

maintain such a great tan
odybuilders seem so dark
ryone lives in Florida or
you do it?

A: Like most competitive bodybuilders, I use a combination of natural sun, sun-tanning beds, and coloring capsules and a special skin-coloring dye. Even the lucky

Floridians, Californians, and Hawaiians use this regimen.

There's debate over the best way to obtain a suntan. Too much exposure to regular sunlight is not good. Both the burning and tanning rays of the sun damage your skin, although the burning rays are more damaging. Skin cancer can develop with too much exposure. And, there's substantial evidence suggesting that skin cancer is more likely in people who suffered severe blistering burns as youths.

Light from sun-tanning beds is safer, but there is some scientific concern that this might be dangerous, too. Still, bodybuilders use booth and regular sunlight to prepare for a contest. I just don't recommend that people spend more time in them than they have to.

Tanning pills are combinations of various food-coloring dyes, all of which have been approved by the Food and Drug Administration. *However, the FDA has not officially approved the use of this dye in any capacity other than as a food-coloring factor.* Thousands of these capsules and pills have been used, though, to help produce that much desired contest color. I use them myself before a contest. They won't make you really dark, but they will provide a nice base of color. It takes about two weeks before they work and once you stop taking them, the color they have produced fades away in about 5–10 days. You probably should only use them before a contest.

There are other types of pills available only by prescription. These are the dangerous ones and I suggest you leave them alone.

I also use a commercial skin-coloring dye called Fast Tan. It's safe and inexpensive. More importantly, it's very effective. It produces a natural-looking deep tan color that is not orange-looking or chocolate-looking. Bodybuilders use other products, too, like Coppertone Sudden Tan, QT, and Clinique Instant Bronzer Lotion. Not all bodybuilders have the luxury of lounging about in ole sol, yet, we are tan year round. Now you know the reason why!

Q: *Do bodybuilders shave all their body hair? If so, why? What is the best way to remove it?*

A: Bodybuilders don't have to shave. There's no rule requiring that they shave before a competition. However, all male bodybuilders do, because a body devoid of excess hair looks much more defined underneath the posing lights. This is the only reason they shave and believe me, they wouldn't if they didn't need to!

Some bodybuilders use special hair-removing creams or wax treatments, but most opt for the old razor. Creams aren't effective for everybody, especially extremely hirsute individuals. Light-haired men can use creams. Some men develop rashes from these depilatories. If men do use the creams, they start early to remove all the hair they can and then they finish the process with shaving.

Wax hair removal is expensive and somewhat painful, but is gaining in popularity because it's a fast process performed by professionals. However, bodybuilders haven't taken to this process too much, since they have so much hair to remove it makes waxing a bit impractical.

Bodybuilders with fine hair can use cheap disposable blades. Coarser-haired men need to use a sharp commercial blade such as the platinum-plus blade. Another popular razor is the kind professional trainers use to shave football players' ankles prior to taping.

Bodybuilders start shaving at least 10 days
selve:
shoul
sever
of yo
grain
and
startii
initial
stubb

A fi

A:
surg
erens,
tion still
devoid of
been permanent
Vasectomy is
trol. Should you de
ever, the vas deferen

Q: *How can I tell if my training partner would be a good match for me in mixed pairs couples bodybuilding competition? How should we prepare for this?*

A: Generally, you should both be at the same level of muscle development, relative to your sex differences. One of you can't be world-class caliber if the other is a novice. You need comparable muscle development.

Your frames should harmonize. If you are very tall, your partner should be tall as well. If you are stocky, he should be, too.

Personality is a consideration. You must be able to give and work together. You need to make concessions. You may like a pose while your partner hates it. Someone has to give. You need a lot of energy. Not only do you need to train like devils, but couples competition requires extra work on posing.

What about permission? Maybe I'm putting the cart before the horse! If you are not posing with your spouse or your girlfriend or boyfriend, is everybody cool about it?

Once those aspects are taken care of, it's time to work on specifics. To prepare, train and diet exactly as you would for a singles competition. Try to develop the corresponding muscle definition and/or size as your partner. Work on your posing, both relaxed and mandatory positions. Once you start to know each other, go to work on your couples routine. Practice everything as a unit because that is what you are. Your posing routine will count 50% in your final score. It must be fluid and show your development. Practice, practice, practice! Good luck.

Q: *My husband works out regularly. He is thinking about getting a vasectomy. Will this prevent him from gaining muscle?*

No. A vasectomy is an operation where a ~~on~~ removes or severs a man's vas def- ~~he~~ tube that carries sperm. Ejacula- ~~takes~~ place, but the ejaculate is ~~perm,~~ because the sperm has ~~tly~~ detoured.

~~good~~ form of birth con- ~~sire~~ children later, how- ~~s~~ would have to be

reconnected surgically. It's very often impossible to restore this function. So don't make the decision lightly.

I know of no anatomical or physiological reason why this operation should prevent your husband from developing muscle. The testicular function is not damaged, so he will continue to produce just as much muscle-building testosterone as before. Likewise, there should be no changes in his sex drive.

There will be some tenderness following surgery, but once that is gone, he should resume his workouts with the same intensity as before. Some men have experienced transient psychological problems with their sexuality following vasectomy, but only because they haven't understood that this operation does not make them any less a man!

Q: *People in the gym tell me I have to do Squats to thicken my thighs. I've heard that they wreck your knees. Your opinion?*

A: Any lifting exercise can be dangerous if you use lousy technique! Squatting improperly can damage your knees and your back.

However, if you squat correctly, it's a great exercise.

Never do a full Squat without *total control*. Never *drop* into a full Squat position. Never *relax* in a full Squat position. Always descend under total control and return to a standing position under total control.

In a deep Squat position, there's some stretch placed on your knee ligaments. However, if the stretch is slow and static rather than dynamic, there is no damage done. However, I don't think it's really necessary to do *full* Squats!

You can get the same thigh-building effect from parallel Squats. Squat down until your thighs are parallel to the floor and then come back up. This still works all the big muscles in your back, thighs, and hips without exposing your knee ligaments to any unnecessary stretching.

Incidentally, most people hurt their backs when squatting rather than their knees. When you squat, you should try to keep your back as flat and upright as possible. Bearing the weight of the bar directly over your spine is the best way to squat. You can do this only by maintaining an upright position.

Squats are a good exercise, but not everybody needs to do them or can tolerate them. You can build thick thighs by working hard on Leg Presses, Hack Squats, Leg Extensions, Leg Curls, and Lunges. If you do decide to give Squats a go, then start with an empty bar! Learn the proper technique first and chances are you won't have to worry about injuries.

Q: *Help! I'm training for a contest and I just don't have any energy. My calories are low because I've got to get defined. I tried coffee because friends said it would help, but I got jittery and spaced-out. I never drink it otherwise. Where do bodybuilders get their energy without turning into java junkies?*

A: Your reaction is typical of non-coffee drinkers. Caffeine affects everyone differently depending on your age, the amount of food in your stomach, your body weight, and your caffeine tolerance.

Caffeine is a central nervous system stimulant. Most people handle about 5–7 milligrams of pure caffeine per kilogram of body weight before they "space-out" or get jittery. So, if you weigh 80 kilograms (176 pounds), you can safely consume about three heaping cups of the black brew. Of course, adding sugar makes your buzz worse!

There are approximately 400 milligrams of caffeine in three cups of regular coffee. By comparison, a glass of tea contains 60 milligrams, a glass of cola about 60 milligrams, and a No-Doz tablet supplies 100 milligrams of caffeine.

Caffeine's effects are cumulative. Caffeine does seem to help your supply of energy. Tests done with marathon runners indicate that caffeine helps to mobilize stored fats from the liver. These fats can then be utilized for energy in long-distance races. Whether it helps a bodybuilder is questionable.

To be perfectly honest, I used to drink 2–3 cups before training, but now it gives me heartburn. I do occasionally use guarana, an herbal caffeine derivative indigenous to South America. It works for me. I should point out that the new drug tests in competitive bodybuilding might eventually forbid caffeine, but the amount forbidden is a lot, as much as is contained in eight cups of coffee!

I think you should look at your diet again. It's normal to get tired when you diet for a show. However, I think bodybuilders routinely cut their carbohydrates too low. Carbs are your main energy source, protei...

Add... Fruits, ... provid... calorie... breads, ... long-te... a comp... carboh... adequa... a lot of... fat!

Q: *I've been accused of using anabolic steroids because I have some facial hair. I don't. It's not dark, but it's noticeable. What's the cause and how can I get rid of it?*

A: Visit an endocrinologist. This is a doctor specializing in hormonal imbalances in your body. You may have some kind of hormone imbalance, but because the hair is not dark, I tend to doubt this.

Plenty of women have this sort of peach fuzz. Most of them have never even heard of anabolic steroids! How do they deal with it? By removing it, that's how!

Methods of facial hair removal can be painful and most of them are only temporary. The damn hair just seems to keep coming back, no matter what you do.

You can attempt to bleach or wax your hair away. Or, if you have the pain tolerance of a karate expert, you can turn to the time-honored tweezers! Ouch! These somewhat primitive methods actually seem to work best, but they must be repeated every few weeks.

To get rid of this hair permanently, you have to destroy both the hair and its root. This can be accomplished through electrolysis. An expert has to perform this procedure. Should your endocrinologist suggest this, it might be the way to go.

Q: *I'm 25 and four months pregnant. I enjoy pumping iron. Can I continue working out or should I stop now? I love being in shape, but I don't want to harm my baby.*

A: I agree with experts who say some exercise is good for expectant mothers. Women who exercise during pregnancy have easier deliveries and shorter labor. They also seem to recover their muscle tone following pregnancy much faster.

Many pregnant women suffer back pain. Extra weight in the abdomen causes the hip. Back muscles contract to prevent and then go into spasms. If you have adequate muscle tone to control of the pelvis, you can put on your back discs and

The way to control pelvic tilt is to develop abdominal strength and hip flexibility. Exercise will do this. I suggest moderate activity (walking, swimming, bike riding, but not fast jogging) up through your seventh to eighth month. You also should continue doing muscle-toning exercises up to this time. Don't push yourself too hard. You won't have the aerobic capacity you had before you became pregnant. Also be aware that your hip joints will be loosening a bit and you won't have the same coordination and control of your movements that you had before.

Gradually decrease your workout intensity as delivery time draws near. When you do your abdominal exercises, don't lie flat on your back. Theoretically, this position could interfere with blood flow to the baby. This is most important during the last trimester when your body weight is at its highest point. Take it easy and be cautious, but continue to exercise. You'll be healthier and so will your baby.

Q: *How do you know when you've gone stale? I've been bodybuilding for a year, but over the last six months I haven't made any progress. I use heavy weights and do a lot of forced repetitions. Still, I don't see any pump or increase in strength. Maybe I'm not cut out to be a bodybuilder.*

A: Maybe you're not cut out for the type of workout you're doing! I'd say you're stale, maybe even overtrained.

I've discussed overtraining elsewhere in this book, but I'll reiterate some points. Many bodybuilders try to do too many sets and exercises. Many bodybuilders use weights that are way too heavy for them. *Most* bodybuilders don't gain anything from forced repetitions and, in fact, tend to burn out from them!

Understand that your nervous system has its limitations. Too much stress is not good, whether it be mental, physical, or emotional. Training with very heavy weights all the time and doing forced repetitions may be burning you out. Your body needs to be coaxed, not blasted!

How to improve your condition? Try to get more sleep and relaxation away from the gym. Eat well and use supplements—change your training venue.

Perhaps you should change your routine all around. Are you training six days a week? Maybe four would be better. Are you doing a double-split routine? Maybe working out just once a day would suit you better.

I've discussed repetitions in my book, but I believe most bodybuilders make their best gains doing between 8–15 reps; some people need to go even higher. Bodybuilders get brainwashed reading about super-duper, super-intense, heavy workouts.

Stress muscle isolation instead of using heavy weights. If you cheat the weight up, you cheat your muscles, too.

I'll outline one of the ways I prefer to train:

- *Set one:* Use a light weight for 20 reps.
- *Set two:* Use a heavier weight for 15 reps.
- *Set three:* Use a heavier weight for 10–12 reps.
- *Set four:* Use a heavier weight for 10–12 reps.
- *Set five:* Repeat the procedure for set four.
- *Set six:* Decrease your weight for 10–12 reps.
- *Set seven:* Decrease your weight for 15–20 reps.

This method of training practically *guarantees* growth.

Finally, if you want to grow and gain, you must eat. Try to eat four or five times a day, with each meal properly spaced apart. Supplement your diet with a vitamin-mineral preparation and drink at least 8–10 glasses of water each day.

Try my changes in your routine and diet and you won't be stale for long!

Q: *Is there any way I can get taller? I'm 13, but I'm just barely 4'8" tall. Is there a food or pill to make me taller? Will bodybuilding make me taller?*

A: I don't think you are finished growing. Thirteen is still pretty young and you may find that you can grow another 4–5 inches.

Height is genetically determined. It's hard to say how tall you will be because you didn't tell me the heights of your grandparents or parents. You can estimate, though. Provided you are healthy, you should expect to be two inches taller than your maternal grandmother and 1–2 inches taller than your mother, if your father is 5'11" or taller. If your father is shorter than average you may not reach the full height of your grandmother or mother.

Right now you are entering a critical growth age. If you are a slow maturer, you can expect to get taller. If you've already done a significant amount of maturing, you may not get much taller. I reached my full height when I was 16.

Unless you are deficient in certain critical enzymes, vitamins, or proteins necessary for genetic growth, there is no miracle food or pill that will increase your height. You should eat a balanced diet with adequate protein. If you are really concerned about your height, your doctor can check you and tell you if there's anything that might be limiting your height. Right now, you are not that far away from average for your age group.

Stretching and bodybuilding exercises can stimulate growth, however, there's no direct link between exercise and linear growth. In other words, exercise does not make your bones longer. However, if you have a postural deformity, such as curvature of your spine (and that's fairly common with girls your age), exercise can help correct that and, indirectly, increase your height!

Doctors use growth hormones to stimulate height in those individuals who have a glandular deficiency. I doubt that this is your concern as a deficiency would have been found long ago.

Don't be too concerned about your height. After all, Mary Lou Retton, the great gymnast, is also 4′8″ and she won the 1984 Olympic Games!

Q: *I was told by a judge that I lost my last competition because I was holding too much water under my skin. He said I wasn't fat, just watery-looking. Before the show I was strict with my diet and trained very hard. I did a lot of aerobics and had removed a good deal of visible fat. I wasn't having my period and I didn't junk out at all*

before the show, yet I still was told I retained water. Would diuretics help next time? Are they safe to use?

A: I've always felt that water cannot be completely compartmentalized in the body. If you have a certain amount of water within your muscles, you will have a certain amount under your skin. As a fluid necessary to the function of your body, water is free to travel anywhere throughout your body and chances are, you cannot completely remove much water from one place in your body without removing it in other places as well. However, I do think sweating—via exercise and heat—is a safer way to lose water than are drugs.

Since you brought them up, I'll use diuretics as an example. When you take a prescription water pill you start to urinate. These pills prevent reabsorption of fluid that normally would go back in through your intestinal walls to all places in your body. Instead, water is voided away. Along with it, valuable minerals in the urine are lost. Because this water is not reabsorbed to where it's needed, your body suffers certain diuretic side effects.

- Losing potassium and water from your heart vessels can cause a heart attack!
- Losing water and minerals from your muscles can cause severe cramps!
- Losing water from your brain can cause dizziness and confusion.

Diuretics are very strong drugs. They are used in medical conditions where the patient needs to lose fluid as a lifesaving mechanism. For example, if a person's heart fails to pump blood properly, his lungs can fill with fluid. This can cause severe respiratory distress, a sort of drowning in your own body fluids. Diuretics are necessary to get rid of this water.

Unsupervised, diuretic use is potentially fatal! Stay clear of them. If you seem to be holding water, blame it on your eating and training preparations! Learn from your experience. If you honestly think that some water loss would help, then do it the safe way—by sweating it off with exercise and heat.

Q: *No matter what I do, I just can't seem to get my calves to grow. Right now I train them daily, but they don't go anywhere. I use heavy weights and do 6–8 reps on every set but nothing happens. Do you have any tips for me?*

A: One thing's for sure, there are a lot of people who can't seem to get their calves to grow. Your problem is not at all unusual.

Experience tells me that different body parts respond differently to weight, sets, and reps. In other words, I think hamstrings, calves, and forearms need higher reps to grow. Why is this? I'm not sure it's even true for everyone, but it is for me. I believe that postural muscles, or muscles that contract continually (neck, calves, forearms, low back, etc.) require some sort of unusual stimulation to grow. If you are used to doing high reps, then low reps might shock the muscle into growth. Conversely, in your case, perhaps high reps might better stimulate your calves.

14
THE COMPLETE
MS. OLYMPIA WORKOUT PROGRAM

The following pages present my complete program in summary form. Sets, reps, and exercises for each body part are listed. Study each individual chapter for complete details!

Bodybuilding is form and function. Bodybuilding has made me more athletic and flexible. I can do things now that I never could before, even as a champion track athlete. "Like what?," you ask. Like going for two hours straight in an activity that is both aerobic and anaerobic. Like lifting close to twice my body weight in the Squat 10 times. Like jumping higher and moving quicker than I ever could before.

The ultimate confirmation of what bodybuilding can do is found in the pictures accompanying my thoughts. Flexibility and athleticism are traits much admired in our society. Cultivate them well, for they will serve you well!

MONDAY & FRIDAY
Morning (Chest & Abdominals)

Exercise	Sets	Reps
Low-Incline Dumbbell Presses	5	10–20
High-Incline Dumbbell Presses	5	15–20
Flat-Bench Dumbbell or Barbell Presses	5	8–10
Cable Crossovers or Dumbbell Flyes	4	15–20
Pulldown Crunches	3–4	25–40
Decline Sit-Ups	3–4	100
Leg Raises Off Bench	3–4	10–40
45-Degree Twists	3–4	50–100
Crunches	3–4	40–80

Do the last five exercises as a giant set.

Evening (Back)

Exercise	Sets	Reps
Support Rows with Dumbbells or Barbell	5	10–30
Long Pulley Rows	5	8–20
Lat Pulldowns to the Rear	5	10–15
Lat Pulldowns to the Front with a Straight Bar or V-Handle	5	8–15
One-Arm Dumbbell or Bent-Over Barbell Rows	5	10–15

TUESDAY
Morning (Quadriceps & Abdominals)

Exercise	Sets	Reps
Squats	8	10–20
Hack Squats	4–5	10–15
45-Degree Leg Presses	6–7	10–15
Leg Extensions	6	10–25
Lunges with Barbell or Dumbbells	4	12–15
Pulldown Crunches	3–4	25–40
Decline Sit-Ups	3–4	100
Leg Raises Off Bench	3–4	10–40
45-Degree Twists	3–4	50–100
Crunches	3–4	40–80

Again, do the last five exercises (for the abs) as a giant set.

Evening (Hamstrings, Calves, & Lower Back)

Exercise	Sets	Reps
Lying Leg Curls	8	10–25
Standing Leg Curls	6	10–20
Donkey Calf Raises	4	15–25
Standing Calf Raises	4	15
Seated Calf Raises	3	15
Hyperextensions	4	15–20

WEDNESDAY & SUNDAY
Morning (Shoulders & Abdominals)

Exercise	Sets	Reps
Standing or Seated Dumbbell Presses	7	10–20
Behind-the-Neck Presses	5	8–20
Bent-Over Lateral Raises	4–5	10–15
Standing Lateral Raises	4–5	10–15
Upright Rows or Front Dumbbell Raises	4–5	10–15

Do the last three exercises as a tri-set.

Exercise	Sets	Reps
Pulldown Crunches	3–4	25–40
Decline Sit-Ups	3–4	100
Leg Raises Off Bench	3–4	10–40
45-Degree Twists	3–4	50–100
Crunches	3–4	40–80

Do the abdominal exercises as a giant set.

Evening (Biceps & Triceps)

Exercise	Sets	Reps
Standing Barbell Curls	6	10–20
Standing or Seated Alternate Dumbbell Curls	5	10–20
Scott Curls with a Barbell or Dumbbells	4–5	10–12
Dumbbell Concentration or Cable Curls	4	12–15
Triceps Pushdowns (elbows in)	3	10–15
Triceps Pushdowns (elbows out)	3	15–20
Lying Triceps Extensions	3	12–15
Standing Dumbbell Extensions	3	10–15
Triceps Kickbacks	3	15

SATURDAY
Morning (Quadriceps & Abdominals)

Exercise	Sets	Reps
Squats	5	15–20
Leg Extensions	5	15–20

The above exercises are supersetted.

Smith Machine Squats	5	10–15
Hack Squats	4	10–15
Leg Extensions	3	20
Lunges	3	15–20
Pulldown Crunches	3–4	25–40
Decline Sit-Ups	3–4	100
Leg Raises Off Bench	3–4	10–40
45-Degree Twists	3–4	50–100
Crunches	3–4	40–80

Do the abdominal exercises as a giant set.

Evening (Hamstrings, Calves, & Lower Back)

Exercise	Sets	Reps
Standing Leg Curls	4–5	12–20
Lying Leg Curls	4–5	12–20
Donkey Calf Raises	4	15
Standing Calf Raises	4	15
Seated Calf Raises	4	15
Hyperextensions	4	12–20

DEVELOPING FLEXIBILITY

There is no secret to great flexibility, nor does building muscles impair flexibility. Flexibility is obtained through vital movement. Life is movement. You can make a flexibility program fun. You can practice contorting your body in all kinds of directions, just like a little child does.

I like being a little kid at heart. I'm playful by nature. I also know, like great yoga masters, that moving my limbs through their maximum range of motion at least once a day, makes me healthier, makes my connective tissue more supple, and makes me feel more vital and alive.

Swimmers understand this, and so do martial arts performers. Participants in both sports move their limbs through wide ranges of motion as part of practicing their sport. Sometimes static stretching can be boring, so be athletic! Run, jump, and play your way through life!

If you do want to increase your flexibility, study the pictures on pages 185–193. Take each body part, one by one, and move it into a position where a mild discomfort is felt. Don't go any farther. Just hold it there for 10 seconds. Imagine yourself lying in a sailboat, on a gentle ocean with a warm, tropical breeze caressing your body. Relax. Think pleasant thoughts. Let the world rush by. Pay no attention to it. Your body will relax. You'll become more flexible. After 10 seconds, let up and then repeat the position a couple more times.

Move into a different position for a different body part. Make sure you stretch your hip flexors (quadriceps), hip extensors (hamstrings), back extensors (low back muscles), chest, shoulder, wrist, and arm muscles. Stretch your ankles and outer hip muscles. When you're done imitating all my positions (at least, to the best of your ability—be patient), get up and do a few jumps into the air, run in place a bit, or go for a brisk walk.

Have I asked a lot from you in my book? Yes and no. I've asked you to exercise and to eat right. That might be a lot if you've never done these things before. However, once you change your lifestyle and actually start doing them, you'll fall in love with bodybuilding. You'll see that I'm not really asking anything at all. Falling in love was never so easy. It'll be form and function all the way!

Leg Stretch—Start.

Leg Stretch—Finish.

Open Lunge into Quadricip Stretch—Start.

Open Lunge into Quadricep Stretch—Middle.

Open Lunge into Quadricep Stretch—Finish.

Splits—Advanced flexibility routine that should be performed slowly and carefully.

Straddle Splits—Right; while sitting stretch your legs as far apart as is comfortable and slowly lean to the right and then to the left side as far down as possible, which works the muscles of the inner and outer thigh and sides of the torso.

Straddle Splits—Front.

Straddle Splits—Left.

Ankle and Quadricep stretch.

Arm and Quadricep Stretch—Start.

Arm and Quadricep Stretch—Finish.

Standing Torso Stretch.

Flexibility Freestyle—Open-Arm march.

Flexibility Freestyle—Open Mule Kick.

Flexibility Freestyle—Straddle Jump.

PARTING THOUGHTS

It's spring now. Spring is a time when flowers bloom. The air changes from cold to mild. Spring is a time for rebirth, for growth, for awareness, for life.

Put yourself into a warm breeze, out in the middle of a grassy field. There's a blue sky above and green all around you. Listen to the birds. Listen to your heart.

Listen to that beat, get in touch with yourself. Feel your body. Feel your muscles contract as they move you along, effortlessly, through the field. Do you feel good?

Do you understand, if just for a moment, what it feels like to be in touch with yourself, to appreciate movement?

The bodybuilder knows what I mean. Bodybuilders are in touch with their physical selves and they like how it feels. It feels good. You will know this when you try bodybuilding. You will love how it feels.

It's spring. It's time to bloom. It's time to be reborn. To bodybuilding and all that it gives me and can give you.

Cory Everson

THE SUPERFLEX GLOSSARY

Abdominals: A group of four muscles on the anterior body wall that collectively flex your upper body forward and sideways, rotate your upper body, assist in breathing and stabilization of the torso. Includes the rectus abdominis, internal and external obliques, and transversus abdominis.

Abduction: A lateral movement away from basic anatomical position. Taking your leg out to the side is leg abduction.

Adduction: Movement of an abducted body part back to anatomical position.

Advanced Trainee: Anyone who has actively been bodybuilding correctly for more than a year.

Aerobic: Exercise requiring oxygen in metabolic chains in producing energy. Long-enduring, sustained exercise involving large muscle groups.

Anaerobic: Exercise requiring the splitting of ATPs and glycolysis (breakdown of glucose). Does not require oxygen in this energy-producing metabolic chain. Exercise of a short duration.

Antagonist: The muscle in direct opposition to the prime mover. When the biceps contracts, the triceps acts as the antagonist and relaxes.

Atrophy: Decrease in muscle size.

ATP: Adenosine Triphosphate, a chemical substance providing energy to the muscle cell.

Bar: The iron or steel shaft connecting the weight plates on a barbell set.

Barbell: The iron bar plus the weights and collars holding them in place. An Olympic bar with collars weighs 55 pounds.

Basal Metabolic Rate: The energy needed by the body at complete rest.

Beginner: Any trainee with less than six months' experience.

Biceps: Upper arm muscle that flexes or brings the forearm toward the shoulder.

Blood Pressure: Pressure exerted against the vessel walls by the blood. Measured during contraction (systolic) and relaxation (diastolic).

Bodybuilding: The application of progressive overload to improve the body appearance. Organized competition where athletes are judged on muscle shape, proportion, symmetry, muscularity, definition and posing ability.

Body Fat Percentage: The proportion of a person's total weight that is fat.

Brachialis: A muscle assisting in flexion of the forearm toward the shoulder. Is its strongest when acting with the hand in mid-position.

Brown Fat: Adipose tissue high in mitochondria and well-perfused with blood. Brown fat appears to actually burn calories. The higher percentage of brown fat you have, the faster your metabolism may be.

Calorie: Basic unit of energy measurement; the amount of heat necessary to raise the temperature of one liter of water one degree centigrade.

Canthaxanthin: An FDA-approved food-coloring dye. Bodybuilders take it to produce a tan skin color.

Carbohydrates: One of the three major energy nutrients. Composed of various sugars and starches with different numbers of carbons.

Cholesterol: A blood lipid with a molecular structure analogous to alcohol.

Circuit Training: A bodybuilding system where you do a series of different exercises, one right after another, without rest intervals between exercises.

Contraction: Muscles utilizing energy and expending heat to produce movement of a bone. *Isometric contraction* means maximum force, but without movement. *Isotonic contraction* is movement with a constant tension or unchanging resistance. *Isokinetic contraction* is a movement with constant velocity. *Eccentric contraction* is movement where the muscle resists gravity while lengthening.

Couples Competition: Bodybuilding competition in which a man and woman team to compete against other such pairs. Posing routines comprise 50% of the final score.

Cramping: Various stages of muscle contraction. When the muscle goes into a contraction involuntarily, it cramps. Can be a minor twitch or a major contraction that is quite painful.

Cutting Up: The process of dieting and exercising faster and harder (and more often!) to burn calories, all of which gets rid of body fat.

Definition: The absence of fat concomitant with maximum muscle development.

Delts: Short for *deltoids*. This muscle covers your shoulder joint. It has three separate heads (anterior, middle, and posterior). Its prime functions are shoulder joint flexion, abduction, and extension, although it assists in several other shoulder joint movements.

Density: The thickness of actin-myosin muscle filaments within the muscle. Dense muscles are heavy and hard-looking to the educated eye.

Diabetes: Medical condition where you don't produce insulin or the insulin you do produce is ineffective in transporting blood sugar into the muscle cells.

Diastolic Blood Pressure: Blood pressure within your vessels when your heart is relaxed, or between beats.

Double-Split System: Master trainer Joe Weider's term for morning and evening workouts. Or, simply, working out twice per day.

Dumbbell: A 10–14 inch bar and collars, often one cast unit, used in one hand for exercise.

Eccentric: Refers to a form of muscle contraction. The muscle contracts in an anti-gravity fashion, lengthening as it fights the resistance down. Also called retro-gravity contraction and negatives.

Endurance: The ability to carry on a series of contractions or the ability to supply enough energy and oxygen to the tissues to continue sustained exercise or work.

Energy: The force that sustains life and carries out all involuntary and voluntary work. Expressed in calories of heat.

Enzymes: Substances that speed up the rate of reactions.

Essential Fat: Fat within our major body organs. Essential fat is life-sustaining and rather impervious to caloric restriction and exercise.

Estrogen: The major female sex hormone.

Exercise: To train in an organized, progressive fashion. As a noun, exercise refers to an actual movement, such as curls.

Extension: Return of a body part from a flexed position to normal position. For example, lower leg extensions on a quadriceps machine.

Fast Tan: Commercial product used by body-builders for the ultimate, deep, dark color for competition.

Fast Twitch: Refers to the chemical composition and nerve supply of white muscle fibers. These fibers generate tension very rapidly.

Fat: A basic energy nutrient, when stored in and on the body, called adipose tissue.

Flexibility: Measured in degrees, flexibility is the range of motion of the various body joints.

Flexion: Movement of a body segment away from anatomical position, such as shoulder joint flexion, or bringing a distant segment closer to the center, such as flexion of the forearm to the shoulder. In flexion movements, the insertion of the muscle moves closer to the muscle origin.

Forced Reps: Assisted repetitions.

Giant Sets: A series of four or more exercises grouped together. A trainee does one set of each exercise in back-to-back fashion. An advanced training principle developed by Joe Weider.

Glucose: A common sugar found in the body. Blood glucose stored in the muscles is called *glycogen.*

Glutes: The gluteus muscles. Includes maximus, minimus, and medius. The major function of the glutes is to extend the hip joint.

Hams: Short for hamstrings. Also called the thigh biceps. The hamstrings do knee joint flexion and assist in hip joint extension.

Hemoglobin: Oxygen-carrying blood-born molecule.

Holistic Training: Advanced Joe Weider body-building system referring to a wide variety of repetitions to stress all the elements of the muscle cell.

Hypertension: High blood pressure; usually, beyond 140/90 millimeters of mercury.

Hyperextensions: Beyond anatomical extension. Refers to an exercise where you lie prone and lift your body up beyond extension.

Hypertrophy: Enlargement of the muscles.

Hyperplasia: Refers to splitting of individual muscle fibers.

IFBB: International Federation of Bodybuilders, the world's largest bodybuilding organization for professional and international amateur competition.

Instinctive Training: Training by intuitive feel. A Weider technique that involves understanding your body responses so you know when to change exercises, reps, and sets.

Insulin: A chemical transporting blood sugar into the muscle cells.

Intensity: Percentage of maximum capability or any measure of how hard one works. Single-minded focus.

Intercostals: A group of muscles in between the ribs that assist in respiration.

Intermediate: Refers to a trainee with more than six months but less than a year's bodybuilding experience.

Joint: Connecting area for different body segments where bones come together.

Judging: Systematic measurement or scoring of bodybuilding contestants using a round system. Includes muscularity, symmetry and posing rounds.

Kilocalorie: Internationally accepted measure of energy expenditure; also called *calorie.*

Lactic Acid: By-product of exercise and anaerobic metabolism.

Lifting Belt: A leather belt worn about the waist when exercising. It supports your abdominal contents and lower back and equalizes abdominal pressure.

Lipids: Another name for blood fat.

Lipolysis: The surgical removal of adipose tissue through suctioning techniques.

Lipoproteins: A complex of fat and protein. High density is the "good" kind and low density, the "bad" kind. Both are forms of cholesterol.

Lordosis: Anterior tilting of the pelvis and spine. Specifically, a diagnostic name for a low back medical condition.

Mass: The thickness, size, and density of a muscle.

Maximum Oxygen Uptake: The greatest amount of oxygen that can be taken into the body via the lungs and transported to the working muscle cell. Also called Vo² Max.

Metabolism: The chemical process of ingesting foodstuffs and the resultant chemical changes that occur to utilize those foods for energy and all bodily processes.

Minerals: Inorganic substances important in human metabolism.

Muscle-Bound: A supposed condition in which muscles become so big the person loses coordination and flexibility. In reality bodybuilders are quite flexible and more coordinated than the average person.

Muscle Pull: A strain or very slight tear of the muscle or its attachments.

Muscle Tone: A state of enhanced muscle shape and contractility. A state of enhanced readiness of the muscle's contraction power.

Muscularity: The combination of muscle size and definition.

Myofibril: The actual muscle filament or individual muscle fiber.

Negatives: Another name for eccentric contractions.

Nutrition: The ingestion and processing of foodstuffs, vitamins, minerals, and enzymes. Also, the study of this process.

Obesity: The state of being overly fat.

Olympic Lifting: Weightlifting involving the two-hand snatch and clean and jerk. The highest amount lifted, within a certain weight division, determines the winner.

Overload: Another name for progressive resistance exercise. Overload usually refers to the weight of the bar, but other forms of overload, like taking less rest between sets, and doing more sets, exist.

Overtraining: Taxing yourself beyond recovery capabilities so that there's either no progress or a decrement in performance.

Peaking: Gradually refining one's physique prior to competition. Also, improving the height of a flexed muscle such as peaking the biceps.

Pecs: Short for *pectorals* (main chest muscles). Pecs refer to your pectoralis major and minor. Their main function is horizontal abduction to the midline and vertical pressing from a supine position.

Pentathlon: Organized track competition consisting of five events. No longer in use as the heptathlon (seven events) has replaced it in track competition.

Physique: Overall, basic body structure or build.

Polyunsaturated Fat: A fat usually liquid at room temperature and able to absorb additional hydrogen into its chemical bonds.

Posing: A skilled demonstration of your physique in both original artful positions and required or mandatory positions. Part of the scoring process in bodybuilding competition.

Posedown: A one-on-one competition in which individuals hit a series of their best poses or hit physique shots requested by the judges.

Power: The ability to exert force in a fast manner. Power is force times distance divided by velocity. Power is a measure of work.

Powerlifting: Organized competition or training consisting of the Squat, Bench Press and Deadlift. In competitive weight divisions, he or she who lifts the greatest combination in all three lifts wins.

Pre-Exhaustion: A training technique in which the prime mover is exhausted in one form of exercise and then is immediately assisted by a secondary mover in a different form of exercise to work the prime mover "beyond exhaustion."

Prejudging: An exhaustive system of judging that occurs before the final competition or regular judging. This is done so that the judges get a more comprehensive look at the bodybuilders. Most of the actual scoring takes place here.

Progression: Gradual increase in the severity of your training. Usually refers to gradually increasing your training weights.

Pronation: The anatomical movement of turning your palms down.

Proportion: Refers to the balanced development of all muscle groups.

Protein: One of the three basic energy groups. The others are fats and carbohydrates.

Pump: The state of total muscle congestion with blood and waste products of contraction. Refers to filling of veins and capillaries at the end state of a series of contractions.

Push-Pull: A form of training in which you work both pushing muscles (such as the pectorals and triceps) and the pulling muscles (such as the biceps and back muscles). You can alternate sets of each or train one group in one session and then in the same workout or later in the same day, train the other, antagonistic body parts. A Weider technique.

Pyramiding: A training technique in which you progressively increase the weight and decrease the repetitions and/or decrease the weight and increase the repetitions.

Quads: Short for quadriceps, a large group of four separate thigh muscles that, together, extend the lower leg and flex the hip joint.

Rectus Abdominis: An abdominal muscle with its prime function being flexion of the spine.

Red Muscle Fiber: A type of endurance muscle fiber that is slow contracting. Has a different nerve supply than white fiber and gives up or utilizes its oxygen supply much slower than white fibers.

Repetition: The actual start to finish performance of any individual exercise.

Rest Interval: The amount of time spent relaxing between each set of exercises. During this time period, the muscle recovers a certain percentage of its maximum contraction power.

Ripped: Another name for being cut-up or very defined. Ripped goes beyond normal *definition*. Also called *shredded*.

Routine: The organized exercise schedule. The organized series of competitive poses.

Said Principle: Refers to the way your body responds in a specific way to exercise. Stands for: Specific Adaptation to Imposed Demands. Exercise adaptation is unique to the type of effort confronting a muscle or your system in general.

Sarcomere: Contractile unit of your muscle fibers.

Sarcoplasm: Another name for the fluid matrix, or cytoplasm bathing the cell nucleus.

Saturated Fat: Fats solid at room temperature. Fully bonded chemically with hydrogen atoms.

Scapula: The wing-shaped bone on each side of your upper back. Many back muscles attach to each scapula. Also called shoulder blade.

Serratus: Muscles which overlie your upper ribs on the sides of your body. Developed by pressing and pullover movements.

Set: A series of repetitions.

Shape: In physique terms, refers to the overall harmony of body symmetry and muscle proportion.

Sissy Squat: An exercise in which you do a Squat holding a barbell behind your body so that it just barely grazes the backs of your calves as you rise up and down.

Smith Machine: A large exercise apparatus with weights attached to the ends of both sides of a self-contained bar that slides up and down on a fixed frame. There are also several safety catches on a Smith machine so that you don't need spotters.

Soleus: Postural calf muscle that lies underneath the thicker, stronger gastrocnemius. The soleus is developed through seated calf raises.

Split System: Working your upper body in one session and your lower body the next or dividing your training up by body parts on different days. You train no more than once a day on a split system.

Spot Reduction: The notion that you can selectively get rid of fat from one or more body sites without removing it from other body sites; scientifically impossible (except surgically).

Spotters: People assigned to grab or catch the bar should you not be able to make a repetition. Especially valuable in performing the Squat and Bench Press.

Steroids: Chemically derived drugs similar to testosterone used to gain muscle mass.

Storage Fat: Adipose tissue that surrounds and protects our inner organs and provides body energy in the form of heat.

Stretching: Taking a muscle-joint segment through, or to its end point, in its range of motion and then gently going a bit beyond that point and holding this position statically for a few seconds.

Strength: The ability to exert maximum force in a single repetition.

Striations: Individual muscle fibers evident underneath the skin in a well-developed and highly defined bodybuilder.

Supersets: An alternating set system for performing different exercises.

Supination: Anatomically, turning your palms up.

Supplements: Additional protein, carbohydrates, minerals, vitamins, and enzymes taken with regular foodstuffs (or taken in place of some foodstuffs).

Symmetry: The geometrical arrangement of parts to a whole. In bodybuilding, symmetry primarily refers to the bone structure.

Tension: The contractile force generated by a muscle. Maximum tension is developed in an isometric contraction at zero velocity. Higher tensions exist in eccentric contractions, but are not direct results of muscle contraction.

Testosterone: The major male sex hormone.

Thrombophlebitis: Deep vein blood clots combined with severe venous irritation and stasis of blood flow. Occasionally can occur in the arterial system.

Training-to-Failure: Performing a set of repetitions until momentary exhaustion is achieved.

Triceps: The major elbow joint extensor muscle.

Triglycerides: Circulating fat particles in the blood.

Tri-Setting: Weider-pioneered bodybuilding technique in which you perform one set each of three different exercises in back-to-back fashion without rest in between.

Two-Joint Muscles: Muscles that cross two joints and functions on each joint. The biceps long head is an elbow joint and shoulder joint flexor.

Valsalva Maneuver: Forced exhalation against a closed glottis (holding your breath and lifting at the same time).

Varicose Veins: Veins that have sagged and lost their function.

Vascularity: The prominence of veins in a highly defined muscle.

Vastii Muscles: The combined vastus lateralis and medialis, two muscles helping comprise the quadriceps.

Ventricles: Chambers of the heart that pump blood into the lung circulation (right ventricle) and the systemic circulation (left ventricle).

Vertebrae: Bones of the spine stacked upon each other which collectively form the spinal column. They are separated by spinal discs and fluid.

Vitamins: Cofactors in metabolic reactions. They are organic substances necessary in very minute amounts for ongoing body functions.

Volume: Refers to the number of sets and frequency of workouts.

Warm-Down: A gradual reduction in the level of exercise intensity so that blood does not pool and lead to diminished cardiac circulation.

Warm-Up: A series of exercises, calisthenics or stretches to elevate the temperature of both the bloodstream and joint-muscle fluids prior to heavy exercise.

White Muscle Fiber: Fast-contracting muscle fibers with a separate nerve and metabolic structure from slow (red) muscle fibers.

White Fat: Another name for common adipose tissue. Also called yellow fat. It is differentiated from brown fat by the mitochondria it contains.

Weightlifting: Generic term for general weight training, bodybuilding, powerlifting, or Olympic lifting. In official circles, weightlifting is synonymous with competitive Olympic lifting.

APPENDIX I

Slim foods	Fat foods
lettuce	ham
cabbage	pork, bacon, veal, lamb
celery	sausage
carrots	smoked meats
beets	hot dogs
sprouts	creamed corn
cucumbers	creamy soups
broccoli	creamy salad dressings
asparagus	butter
spinach	cooking oils
cauliflower	peanut butter
brussels sprouts	jelly-jam spreads
corn	desserts
lentils	2%, whole milk
peas	fruit juices
beans	canned fruits
mushrooms	red meat
tomatoes	cheese
all fresh fruits	all forms of chips
nonfat cottage cheese	french fries, hash browns
nonfat milk	ice cream
diet dressing	chocolate
pasta	pizza
wheat and rye breads	egg yolks
baked or whipped potatoes	condiments
pita bread	dried fruits
muffins	granola
bagels	trail mix
turkey	nuts
de-skinned chicken (breasts)	soft drinks
baked or broiled white fish	wine, alcohol, beer
egg whites	liqueurs, ice cream drinks
whole grains	candy
oatmeal	all fried foods
all vegetables	sweet rolls
diet sodas	honey
ice or hot tea	table sugar
coffee	salt
air-popped popcorn	
liver	
venison	

APPENDIX II

COMMON FOODS AND THEIR CALORIE CONTENT

Breakfast Foods	Calories
Bacon (2 strips)	174
Piece of ham	125
Hash browns	200
Oatmeal with whole milk	250
Raisin bran with whole milk	225
Two sausage links	300
Two pieces toast with butter & jelly	290
Whole grapefruit	80
Biscuit with butter & jelly	325
One-quarter cantaloupe	40
Three-egg omelet	450
Three-egg omelet with cheese	600
"Three-egg" omelet (Egg Beaters)	270
Glass of whole milk	150
Glass of skim milk	90
Cup of coffee	2-3
Cup of tea (sugar & lemon)	26–32
Cup of hot tea (plain)	1–2
Cup of hot chocolate	125
Glass of orange juice	90
Glass of tomato juice	30
Glass of apple juice	80

Lunch and Dinner Foods

Lunch and Dinner Foods	Calories
Fast-food hamburger	500
Fast-food hamburger with cheese	650
Chef's salad	475
Tuna salad with mayo	500
Small sirloin steak with serving of vegetables, roll & butter and rice	525
Medium-sized serving of white fish with vegetables, roll & butter and rice	525
Turkey salad sandwich on wheat bread	475
Tuna salad sandwich on wheat bread	475
Large baked potato with butter	250
Mashed potatoes with butter & gravy	350
Whipped potatoes with gravy (no butter)	125
Average serving of fried zucchini	115
Average serving of cooked carrots	90
4-6 ounces of cottage cheese	90
Ear of corn on the cob (butter)	150
25-30 french fries	450
Serving of green beans	50
Green beans with butter	100
Serving of rice	125
3-4 slices of tomatoes	15–25
Eight ounces of cheese	425
Bowl of turkey noodle soup	110
Bowl of clam chowder	475
Bowl of cream of potato soup	500
Lettuce salad with blue cheese dressing and tomato	350
Lettuce salad with thousand island dressing and tomato	350
Serving of onion rings	450
Bowl of vegetable beef soup	90
Scoop of sherbet	105
Scoop of vanilla ice cream	150
Tapioca pudding	130
Order of tartar sauce	140
Pat of butter	25
Package of saltines (2)	25

APPENDIX III

EXERCISE—CALORIE EQUIVALENCE CHART
Based on a 148 pound woman

Exercise	30 Minutes	60 Minutes
Walking at 2.5 mph over flat terrain	165	330
Walking at 3 mph over hilly terrain	250	520
Jogging at 5 mph over flat terrain	340	685
Swimming (35 sec. laps)	300	600
Cycling at 8 mph	170	345
Racquetball (singles)	360	700
Universal Gym Super Circuit weight training	230	475
Aerobic dance class	300	630
Tennis (singles)	225	445
Golf (walking)	170	340
Cross country skiing	560	1120

Exercise heart rate should be between 125–160 beats per minute on any of these activities for an aerobic training effect.

APPENDIX IV

PERSONALIZED ENERGY (CALORIC) NEEDS
Recommended by the Nutrition Board of the National Academy of Sciences

Age	Sex	Average Daily Caloric Need	Caloric Range
15–18	M	2,800	2,100–3,900
19–22	M	2,900	2,500–3,300
23–50	M	2,700	2,300–2,800
51–75	M	2,400	2,000–2,800
Over 75	M	2,050	1,650–2,450
15–18	F	2,100	1,200–3,000
19–22	F	2,100	1,700–2,500
23–50	F	2,000	1,600–2,400
51–75	F	1,800	1,400–2,200
Over 75	F	1,600	1,200–2,000
Pregnant	F	2,400	2,000–2,800
Nursing	F	2,600	2,300–3,000

Precise requirements depend on height, weight, muscle mass, and activity levels.

INDEX

A

Abdominal Crunches, 65
Abdominals, 63–71
Advanced bodybuilding, 34–37
  arm routines, 98–99
  back routines, 126–29
  chest routines, 83–87
  leg routines, 141–45
  shoulder routines, 112–15
Aerobics, 23–25, 55, 56, 169
Age
  and bodybuilding, 39
  caloric needs for different, 206
Alternate Dumbbell Curls, 93–94
Alzado, Lyle, 111
American Diabetic Association,
  166
Amino acids, 44
Anabolic steroids, 6, 166–67, 174
Anaerobics, 23–25, 55
Anatomy, 6–7
Anorexia, 41
Antagonist, 32–33
Arachidonic acid, 43
Arm Curls, 61
Arm exercises, 89–103
  advanced routines, 98–99
  beginning routines, 92–94
  intermediate routines, 95,
    96–97

Athleticism, 179
Atlas, Charles, 23
ATP (adenosine triphosphate), 51

B

Back exercises, 117–29
  advanced routines, 126–29
  beginning routines, 122
  intermediate routines, 123–25
Back injury, 117–19
  prevention of, 119–20
Barbell Press, 106
Barbells, 27, 89
Basal metabolism, 42, 54
Baxter, Kay, 39
Beauty, 1
Beckles, Albert, 83
Beginning bodybuilding, 28–31
  arm routines, 92–94
  back routines, 122
  chest routines, 75–79
  leg routines, 134–37
  shoulder routines, 107, 108–9
Behind-the-Neck Presses, 106,
  107, 108
Belknap, Tim, 166
Bench Press, 30, 61, 106, 148, 165
Bent-Over Lateral Dumbbell
  Raises, 112

Bent-Over Rows, 121, 122, 126, 165
Biceps, 89, 90
Biceps mania, 90–91
Biking, 55
Biological setpoint, 43
Bionic blood, 11–12
Blood pressure, and weight lifting, 169
Bodybuilding, 2, 23
  acceptance of, for women, 20–21, 23,
  Corrine's personal program, 100–103, 129, 142–45, 180–83
  impact of, on body shape, 3–4, 56
  principles of success in, 26–27
Bodybuilding competition, 152–54
  compulsory poses, 153
  contest attire, 160
  and dieting, 155–58
  free posing, 154
  hair care, 162
  and menstruation, 160–61
  muscularity round, 153
  musical accompaniment, 160
  and personal relationships, 162–63
  prejudging round, 152–54
  skin care, 161–62
  and tanning, 158, 160
Bodybuilding fitness, 1–2
Bodybuilding training, 25
Body fat, amount of, 7
Body growth, 175–77
Bowen, Lori, 16, 18
Brachialis, 98
Breast implantation, 73
Breast reduction surgery, 74
Breasts, 73–87
Breathing, importance of, 29
Brisco-Hooks, Valerie, 132
Brown, John, 16
Brown fat, 45
Bulimia, 41
Buttocks, 53–61, 54–55
Byrne, David, 106

C
Cable Crossovers, 84, 85, 87
Cable Curls, 99, 100
Caffeine, 173
Calves, 177
Calorie(s), 42, 53
  and age, 206
  of common foods, 204–5
  determination of, 49
  and exercise equivalence, 206

Cannula, 49
Canthaxanthin, 160
Carbohydrate depletion, 157
Carbohydrates, 43, 44–45, 46–47, 48, 155–56, 173
  thermic effect of, 45
Cardiovascular fitness, 24
Carnitine, 51
Carotene, 43
Cellulite, 54
Cher, 1
Chest exercises, 73–87
  advanced routines, 83–87
  beginning routines, 75–79
  intermediate routines, 80–82
Chinning, 120
Chin-Ups, 120
Cholesterol, 44
Circuit training, 8
Clean and Jerk, 148
Clinique Instant Bronzer Lotion, 171
Competitive weightlifting, 25
Complex carbohydrates, 46, 47
Complex sugars, 44
Compulsory poses, 152
Concentration Curls, 98, 99, 100
Contest attire, 160–61
Coppertone Sudden Tan, 160, 171
Crunches, 70

D
Deadlifts, 15, 55, 118–19, 121, 148
Decline Sit-Ups, 67
Deltoids, 91, 106, 107, 110
Dennis, Diana, 18, 20, 39
Density, 151
Deprivation, 41
Diabetes, 166
Diana, Deborah, 16
Dietary fat, 44
Dieting, 41. *See also* Nutrition
  and contest preparation, 155–58
  and energy level, 173
  genetic factors, 46
  and liposuction, 49, 50
  maintenance of status quo, 42–44
  and metabolism, 44–46
  and nutritional supplements, 51
  and patience, 47
  and undercover calories, 49
  and weight gain, 165–66
  and the yo-yo syndrome, 42
Diuretics, 177
Donkey Calf Raises, 141, 142
Double-split training, 35, 83, 87, 107, 141

Drugs, 168–69
Dumbbell Extensions, 99, 102
Dumbbell Flyes, 84–85, 87
Dumbbell Front Raises, 115
Dumbbell Presses, 106, 107, 109
Dumbbell Rows, 126
Dumbbells, 27, 89
Dunlap, Carla, 16

E
Electrolysis, 174
Entropy, 53
Ergogenic aids, 6
Essential fats, 7
Evans, Linda, 2
Everson, Cory diet of, 50–51,
    156–58
    personal exercise routine of,
        100–103, 129, 142–45,
        180–83
Everson, Jeff, 3, 11, 15–16, 17, 18,
    19, 30, 132, 147, 162, 168
Exercise
    body response to, 7
    calorie equivalence chart, 206
    correct techniques for, 55–56
    impact of, on the heart, 7–9
External obliques, 64

F
Fast Tan, 160, 171
Fast walking, 55–56
Fat(s), 43, 44–45
    loosing, 7
    turning into muscle, 4–5
    types of, 43
Fat cells, 45–46
Fatigue, 34, 166
Fawcett, Farrah, 2
Femininity, and sensuality, 2–3
Ferrigno, Lou, 106
Fiber, 43
Fight-fat-thighs diet, 61
Flat-Bench Barbell Presses, 82
Flat-Bench Dumbbell Presses, 78
Flat-bench exercises, 87
Flexibility, development of, 179,
    184–93
Fonda, Jane, 2
Food and Nutrition Board of the
    National Academy of
    Sciences, 47–48
Forced repetitions, 36, 174
45-Degree Leg Presses, 139
45-Degree Twists, 69
Free weights, 27
Front Dumbbell Press, 106

G
Gastineaus, Mark, 132
Genetics, 46, 175–76
    and fat distribution, 43
Giant sets, 33, 56, 57, 65
Glucose, 43
Glycogen, 43
Goerner, Herman, 118, 119
Goode, Paul, 117
Growth hormones, 176
Gruwell, Shelley, 16
Guarana, 173

H
Hack Squats, 55, 143, 173
Hair care, and bodybuilding
    competition, 162
Hair removal, 171, 174
Hamstrings, 131
Haney, Lee, 17
Hardness, 151
Heart
    impact of exercise on, 7–9
    impact of weightlifting on, 169
Heart disease, 8
Heart rate, 25
Heavy weights, lifting of, 30
Hemingway, Mariel, 2
High-Incline Dumbbell Presses,
    81
Holistic training, 32, 80, 141
Hyperextensions, 55, 121, 125
Hyperplasia, 29
Hypertrophy, 29
Hypothalamus gland, 43

I
Incline Dumbbell Flyes, 79
Incline Press, 106
Injuries, 37–39
    back, 64, 117–19
Inosine, 51
Instinctive training, 35, 83
Insulin, 46, 166
Insulin coma, 166
Insulin shock, 166
Intermediate bodybuilding, 31–34
    arm routines, 95, 96–97
    back routines, 123–25
    chest routines, 80–82
    leg routines, 138–41
    shoulder routines, 107
Internal obliques, 64
Intrathoracic pressure, 29
Isolation, 26–27, 175
Isometrics, 7

J
Jogging, 44, 56, 132, 149

K

Karate, 23 Kemper, John, 16
Kenady, Doyle, 119
Knee wrap, 135

L

Lactic acid, 31
Latissimus dorsi, 120
Lat Machine Pulldowns, 61, 121,
    126, 165
Lat Pulldowns to the Front, 128
Lat Pulldowns to the Rear, 127
Lauper, Cyndi, 105
Leg Curls, 134, 138, 140, 173
Leg development, 131–45
Leg extensions, 59, 134, 138, 141,
    145, 173
Leg Presses, 55, 134, 138, 173
Leg Raises, 61, 65
Leg Raises off the Bench, 68
Leg exercises
    advanced routines, 141–45
    beginning routines, 134–37
    intermediate routines, 138–41
Lifting belt, 135
Linoleic acid, 43
Linolenic acid, 43
Lipase, 45
Liposuction, 49, 50
Long-chain carbohydrates, 44
Long Pulley Rows, 121, 124, 126
Longs, Howie, 132
Lordosis, 64
Low-Incline Dumbbell Presses,
    77–78
Lunges, 55, 58, 138, 145, 173
Lying Leg Curls, 55, 136, 138
Lying Triceps Extensions, 97–98,
    99

M

Machines, and home use, 27
Martial arts, 23
Maximum oxygen uptake, 25
McLish, Rachel, 19
Men
    life expectancy of, 9
    metabolism of, 9
    natural form of, 4, 6–7
Menstruation, 4
    and bodybuilding competition,
        160–61
Metabolism, 9, 165–66
    definition of, 42
    food and, 44–45
    and maintainance of status
        quo, 42–43
    tricking of, 43–44
Minerals, 43, 44
Monounsaturated fats, 43

Muscalarity, 150, 151–52
Muscle(s), 45
    atrophy of, 4
    rupturing of, 167–68
    turning into fat, 4–5
Muscle & Fitness, 18
Muscle isolation, 26–27, 175
Muscle myths, 4
Muscle priority training, 95
Muscle soreness, 31
Muscle tone, 2, 4
Musical accompaniment, 160–61

N

National Strength Coaches
    Association, 147
"Negative-calorie" foods, 54
Negative training, 36
Neophyte chest training, 75–76
Nutrition, 5–6. *See also* Dieting
    calorie content of foods, 204–5
    listing of slim and fat foods,
        203
Nutritional supplements, 5–6, 51,
    169, 175

O

Olympic weightlifting, 23, 118,
    148. *See also* Weightlifting
    Soviet style of, 132–33
Overtraining, 36, 37, 91, 95, 166,
    174–75
    signs of, 34

P

Pain back, 64, 117–19
    and bodybuilding, 36–37
Patience, need for, in weight loss,
    48–49
Pectoralis major/minor, 75
Pelvic tilt, 175
Personal relationships, and
    bodybuilding competitions,
    162–63
Phlebitis, 13
Pirie, Lynne, 16, 39
Plakinger, Tina, 16
Plastic surgery, and breast size,
    73–75
Polyunsaturated fats, 43
Posing, 150, 152
Postural deformity, 176
Powerlifting, 23, 118, 134, 148
Pregnancy, 174
Prejudging, 152
Principal, Victoria, 2
Progressive overload, 26
Protein, 43, 44, 47–48, 155–56
Pulldown Crunches, 66
Pulldowns, 120–21

Pull-Ups, 120, 121, 126
Push-pull system of training, 111, 129
Push-Ups, 75, 89, 90
Pyramid approach, 32, 87, 99, 111

Q-R
RDA (recommended daily allowance), 47–48
Rectus abdominis, 63, 64
Reeves, Steve, 150
Refined sugars, 46
Relativity, 3–4
Repetitions, 29, 175
Resting heart rate, 8–9
Rest intervals, 37, 141
Retro-gravity training, 36
Retton, Mary Lou, 25–26, 106, 176
Reverse pyramid, 32
Roberts, Mary, 19, 20, 39
Rope jumping, 56
Rowing, 120, 126

S
Salad bars, 49
Saturated fats, 43
Scott Curls, 95, 96, 98, 99
Seated Calf Raises, 138, 141
Seated Press Curls, 165
Sensuality, 1–2
and femininity, 2–3
Serratus muscles, 65, 75
Setpoint, 43
resetting, 45
Sets, 29
Sexuality, 105
Shaving, 171
Shepherd, Cybill, 1, 2
Shorter, Frank, 80
Shoulder Presses, 61
Shoulder shrugs, 75
Shoulders, 105–14
advanced routines, 107, 110–14
beginning routines, 107, 108–9
intermediate routines, 107
Silicone injections, 74
Sit-Ups, 61, 165
Skeletal muscle, 45
Skin cancer, 158, 171
Skin care, and bodybuilding competition, 161–62
Skin elasticity, loss of, 168
Skipping, 56
Smith Machine Squats, 144, 145
Smith Rack Squats, 55
Snacking, 61
Snatch, 148

Soleus muscles, 131
Specificity, 26
Spitz, Mark, 25
Split system of training, 31–32, 107
Sports, bodybuilding as form of, 20–21, 148–50
Spotters, need for, 30
Sprinting, 131
Squats, 30, 55, 57, 134, 138, 141, 145, 148, 165, 172–73
importance of technique, 135
Stair climbing, 55
Standing Barbell Curls, 92
Standing Calf Raises, 137, 141
Standing Curls, 165
Standing Dumbbell Lateral Raises, 113
Standing Leg Curls, 55, 60
Static isometrics, 7–8
Stationary biking, 56
Storage fat, 7
Strength training, 147
Streptokinase, 12
Style, 133–34
Sucrose, 46
Sugar, 46
Supersets, 32–33, 111
Supported Bent-Over Rows, 123
Swayback, 64 Swimming, 56
Symmetry, 150, 151, 165, 169

T
Table sugar, 46
Tan, maintenance of, 170–71
Tanning, 158, 160
Tanning beds, 158, 171
Tanning pills, 171
Technique, importance of, 28
Terminology, 28–29
Testosterone, 4, 6, 9, 106, 167
Thermic effect, 45, 47
Thickness movement, 121
Thighs, 53–61
Thomas, Heather, 2
Thyroid gland, 165
Training frequency, 26
Training intensity, 26
Training log, use of, 30
Training partners
need for, 30
selection of, 172
Training volume, 26
Transversus abdominis, 64
Triceps, 90, 91
Triceps Kickbacks, 99, 103
Triceps Pushdowns, 61, 94, 99
Tri-set, 33, 111

U-V
Upright Rows, 111, 114
Valsalva Phenomenon, 29
Vasectomy, 172
Vitamins, 43, 44

W
Walking, 55
    suggested routine for, 55–56
Warm-up, need for, 28, 37, 38
Water, 43
    consumption of, 61
    retention, 161, 176–77
Weider, Joe, 18, 35, 56, 83
Weight, determination of amount
    of, for lifting, 30
Weight belt, 38–39
Weight classes, 152

Weight gain, dieting for, 165–66
Weightlifting. *See also* Olympic
    weightlifting
    classes in, 148, 152
    competition in, 148
    impact of, on heart, 7–8
Weissmuller, Johnny, 133
Welch, Raquel, 1, 2
Wheeler, Gema, 16
Women
    body building for, 20–21, 23
    life expectancy of, 9
    metabolism for, 9
    natural form of, 6–7

Y
Yo-yo syndrome, 42